D1611806

Rehearsal
for
Disaster

OTHER BOOKS BY JOHN D. HICKS

The Populist Revolt

The Federal Union

The American Nation

A Short History of American Democracy

The American Tradition

Republican Ascendancy, 1921-1933

University of Florida Press
Gainesville - 1961

THE BOOM
AND
COLLAPSE
OF
1919-1920

Rehearsal
for
Disaster

JOHN D. HICKS

BARUCH
BURLESON
COOLIDGE
DEBS
DEWEY
FOSTER
GARY
GOMPERS
HANSON
HARDING
HOOVER
HOUSTON
LAFOLLETTE
LANDIS
LANSING
LEWIS
LUSK
MCADOO
MELLON
PALMER
SACCO
SCHWAB
SMITH
VANZETTI
WILSON

To My Sister
Hattie Hicks Ducker

By Way
of
Introduction

One of the most interesting events of the last few years has been the lectures on American civilization sponsored by the Department of History. This lecture series has included some of the most distinguished historians of our time. It is altogether proper that Dr. John D. Hicks should be part of that eminent group.

Whenever Dr. Hicks speaks or writes about the Midwest and its problems, it is obvious that the great Valley of Democracy has found its strong, clear spokesman. The exciting *Populist Revolt* after thirty years still stands as a monument to Dr. Hicks's insights, scholarship, and ability to make history vital. That he should also be the author of the most popular college texts on American history is quite understandable.

In this series of lectures, Dr. Hicks once more recalls to a rapidly urbanizing society the ferment and torment of a vast farming region in the throes of great change: a farming area that was slowly but inexorably being altered by the overwhelming strength of industrialism. As Dr. Hicks notes, the price of this change was much larger than was commonly understood at the time.

I should like to take this opportunity to express the gratitude of the University of Florida for three enjoyable evenings—and now this collection of lectures. The shadow of Dr. Hicks is long in American historiography. It was an honor to have him with us, even though it was only for a short time.

J. WAYNE REITZ, *President*
University of Florida

REHEARSAL
FOR
DISASTER

The Author's
Personal
Acknowledgments

The three chapters that compose this little volume follow in somewhat expanded form the lectures in American civilization that I was privileged to give at the University of Florida, April 25-27, 1960, on invitation of the University's Department of History. Some interesting parallels between the big boom and collapse of the 1920's, of which I had recently written, and the little boom and collapse of 1919-1920, to which I had given scant attention, gave pretext for the subject. The parallels are by no means exact—historical parallels never are— but perhaps a greater willingness during the 1920's to learn from the experience of history might have served the nation well. Perhaps it still might help.

I want to record my gratitude to the many individuals who made it possible for my wife and me to visit the University of Florida, and whose earnest efforts provided the audiences to which I spoke on three successive evenings.

We particularly appreciated the thoughtful campus courtesies that President J. Wayne Reitz and Dean Ralph E. Page extended to us. Nor shall we soon forget the generous hospitality we received in the homes of Professors L. N. McAlister, Donald E. Worcester, John A. Harrison, Rembert W. Patrick, Arthur W. Thompson, A. Curtis Wilgus, and John K. Mahon, the visit to the P. K. Yonge School that Mrs. Alfred Diamant so kindly arranged for Mrs. Hicks, and the opportunity Mrs. Frank Flanigan gave me to address an assembly of students at the Gainesville High School. I am deeply indebted also to Director and Mrs. Lewis F. Haines of the University of Florida Press for their part in turning my manuscript into so attractive a book, and to Mr. Paul Chalker for his extremely competent editorial guidance.

JOHN D. HICKS

University of California
Berkeley
April, 1961

REHEARSAL
FOR
DISASTER

Table
of
Contents

Business
and
Government

Will Rogers' gibe that the United States has won every war and lost every peace was only a half-truth at most, but it well expressed the despair with which American idealists viewed the events that followed the First World War. A smooth transition from war to peace is rarely achieved, but in this instance the going turned out to be particularly rough. The people had been oversold on what the winning of the war would mean, in part by President Wilson's well-advertised tenets, and in part by their own high hopes. They could see, all too soon, that the world had not yet been made safe for democracy, and that the war to end war had only just begun. They were obliged to witness the fall of the leader on whose words the whole world had so lately hung. They themselves, in the mid-term elections of 1918, had dealt him the first heavy blow. When in a moment of unwonted political ineptitude he had asked for a Democratic Congress, they had responded in fitful irritation by returning Republican majorities in both houses. He was disappointed, no doubt, that in the Paris negotiations he won only a partial victory for his peace program, but the next great blow came when he broke physically under the strain of office, never to be the same man again. Finally the Republican Senate, eagerly pressing its advantage over a fallen foe, turned down the treaty he had fought so hard to win. The decade of cynicism was off to a good start.[1]

The collapse of the President, tragic as it was, by no means equaled in importance the collapse of the Presidency itself. The government of the United States was geared to Presidential leadership; without a powerful President the whole mechanism broke down. This had not always been true. The lingering illness of Garfield, for example, caused little disturbance to the federal government of his time; there was then not enough Presidential power for its absence to be seriously felt. It is true that during our earlier history the nation had occasionally experienced a strong executive, but usually only in an emergency, as when Jackson personified the rise of the common man, or when Lincoln saved the union from destruction. The Presidency as the institution we know today was essentially a twentieth-century creation. Theodore Roosevelt, more than any other individual, set the new pattern, and when his successor, William Howard Taft, tried to retreat to a more conventional view, the people promptly turned him out. Woodrow Wilson, like Roosevelt, tended to exalt the Presidential prerogative, and to fix even more firmly in the public mind the idea of Presidential leadership. This was no less true of the prewar than of the war years. Throughout both periods the Presidency was dominant, and even Congress listened respectfully to the sound of its master's voice.[2]

The vacancy at the top did not come primarily because the Republicans had won the elections of 1918. While this political reversal did mean trouble for the President with the legislative branch, it did not mean any change in his view of his rights and duties. His readiness to assume full authority to act for the United States in the peace negotiations provides ample evidence on that score. What Wilson did not foresee was that the Presidency, with the President long out of the country, could not continue in the character that he and Roosevelt had given it. There was simply too great a concentration of power in the President's hands; too much depended upon his initiative and his ready accessibility. Wilson could and did discharge overseas the treaty-making responsibilities of his office, but on the home front a dangerous vacuum developed. The President was freely criticized for his failure to delegate authority, but many decisions could not be delegated, nor for that matter could the need for them even be anticipated. The result was inaction when action was needed, postponement when only promptness would have sufficed. It should not be forgotten that in these days the President could cross the ocean only by steamship; he had not the easy mobility that air travel later gave Dulles and Eisenhower. Wilson lacked even the advantages of trans-Atlantic telephonic communication. As a result his "conference at the summit" involved a descent to near chaos at home. The old funny magazine, *Life,* pointed up this dilemma in a series of not-so-funny cablegrams addressed to "Wilson, Paris," and signed "The American People." "Please hurry home and look after the labor situation." "Please hurry home and look after the railroads." "Please hurry home and fire Burleson." "Please hurry home. Let someone else do it."

Bad as the President's absence from the country was,

BUSINESS
AND
GOVERNMENT

3

his critical illness, which began only two months after his return, was infinitely worse. He had tried to keep in touch with home affairs while he was abroad, and he had returned to the United States for a brief visit in late February and early March, 1919. But only two months after he brought the Treaty home his health broke. For a while he was half-paralyzed and racked with pain; during this period, with news filtered in to him only through his wife, his physicians, and his private secretary, his work as President went virtually undone. After his partial recovery he could sign or veto bills, hold essential conferences, make official pronouncements, fill appointive vacancies, try in vain to advance the fortunes of the Treaty and the League. But the fact remains that the Presidency, as he once had viewed it, had disintegrated. "To draw the parallel with a ship under full sail, in the midst of a squall, and minus her helmsman, would hardly be a figure of speech, the comparison is so accurate." So the situation appeared to a contemporary observer.[3]

Unfortunately, under the American system the Cabinet could not serve as a substitute for the Presidency. It lacked constitutional authority for its existence, and was only what each individual President chose to make it. Wilson had not chosen to make it very much. Some of the men he had named to Cabinet positions turned out to be effective administrative officers, but he did not in any special way lean on them for advice nor seek to integrate them as a group. Moreover, the end of the war meant a number of Cabinet changes, most of which were not for the better; only four of Wilson's original appointees stayed with his administration the full eight years. While Wilson's illness was at an acute stage, in October, 1919, his Secretary of State, Robert Lansing, called the Cabinet together, quite obviously in order to explore the possibilities of collective action. To Wilson this seemed like an act of insubordination, and his irritation led at length to Lansing's dismissal. Undoubtedly Lansing meant no harm, and yet it must have been quite clear to him, as Wilson pointed out, that the Cabinet without the President could assume authority only by usurpation. Left thus without effective leadership, the Cabinet was more effectively "balkanized" than ever, "with each department head rushing he knows not whither."[4]

If neither the President nor the Cabinet was in a position to provide leadership, the same thing was almost equally true of Congress. After the Civil War, when the President and Congress fell out, Congress scored a knock-out victory over its adversary and took into its own hands the leadership of the nation. But the Congress that defied Andrew Johnson had more than a two-thirds majority in each house opposed to the President, whereas the post-World-War-I Congress could but rarely override a Presidential veto, and then only on such inconsequential matters as the definition of the alcoholic content in intoxicating beverages, and the repeal of daylight-saving time. That Congress was tired to death of executive leadership and eager to thwart the President at every turn was clear enough. But the legislative branch had nothing to offer as a substitute for the deflated Presidency.[5]

Part of this trouble could be traced to Congressional weaknesses more fundamental than the lack of a larger Republican majority. The Senate had become so deeply engrossed in the Treaty fight that it had little time left for anything else. The House was not only short on effective personnel, but by force of habit deferred to the Senate, to which its abler members so often graduated. One trouble with the members of both houses, according to H. L. Mencken, was their close identification with the locally minded political machines on which they depended. Even the Senators could rarely think beyond the boundaries of their individual states, while the Representatives were hemmed in by even narrower constituencies. Men with breadth of vision were no match as office seekers, Mencken argued, for the "small groups of narrow, ignorant, and unconscionable manipulators" who dominated local politics.[6] However that may be, it would have taken courage of a much higher order than Congress possessed to have dealt effectively with the vacancy in the Presidency that Wilson's illness created. At least Congress should have found some means of devolving upon the Vice-President, as the Constitution had anticipated, the duties of an incapacitated President.

As for the once powerful wartime government, the fighting had barely ended when its destruction began. The six great war boards through which the nation had mobilized for victory did not last long. The War Industries Board, which with Bernard Baruch at its head had ruled American business with an iron hand, ceased to exist on January 1, 1919, when Baruch's resignation became effective. In its place an Industrial Board, designed to systematize government buying and to stabilize prices, was created within the Department of Commerce. But the new board lacked authority, and its chairman, George N. Peek, was unable to keep it in existence for more than a few months. The history of the War Trade Board, which in its time had exercised complete control over exports and imports, went through a similar cycle. On June 30, 1919, with lessened powers, it was attached to the Department of State, and on May 27, 1921, it was abolished by act of Congress. Hoover's Food Administration lost much of its reason for existence with the signing of the armistice; on July 1, 1919, Hoover resigned, and on August 21, 1920, the agency folded up. Garfield's Fuel Administration was gone by the end of 1919, and McAdoo's Railroad Administration by March 1, 1920, when the railroads were turned back to their owners. The United States Shipping Board could not be so summarily liquidated, for some organization had to act as custodian for the ships it had built, but by the Jones Merchant Marine Act of 1920 it was given a kind of receiver's mandate to carry on temporarily and find private owners for government merchantmen if it could. What happened to the six principal war boards happened also to the lesser agencies. To a certain extent all this was necessary and proper. What was really alarming was the fact that neither the President nor Congress seemed to realize the need for an effective peacetime government to guide the nation through the difficult years that lay ahead.[7]

It was perhaps too much to expect that a disintegrating government would be able to provide for the orderly demobilization of its military forces. Almost unanimously the American people regarded the winning of the war as the end of the nation's military mission, and demanded that the men in uniform be sent home. Even so, the utter planlessness that characterized the retreat from Europe is hard to forgive. The signing of the armistice was regarded as excuse enough to warrant disbanding the million and a half men in Army camps at home and reversing the direction of traffic on the "bridge across the seas." Pershing's crusaders must come back at once. Complaints from soldiers who were not immediately ordered home were long and loud:

> *We drove the Boche across the Rhine,*
> *The Kaiser from his throne.*
> *Oh, Lafayette, we've paid our debt,*
> *For Christ's sake send us home.*

Public opinion being what it was, the Army, despite the qualms of those in high command, had no choice but to destroy itself as fast as it could; by the summer of 1919 the number of discharges had reached two and three-quarter million, and by the following November, with demobilization officially proclaimed at an end, a half-million more. Various methods of demobilization in accordance with individual needs or employment opportunities were considered, but the "Army way" turned out to be the disbanding of one military unit after another as opportunity offered. Of necessity some American troops had to participate in the Allied march to the Rhine after the armistice and to share the dull business of occupation duty. This assignment fell to the Third Army, which advanced to the Coblentz bridgehead. But the American Expeditionary Forces in Germany, as these troops were renamed, were speedily whittled down to token proportions, and on January 24, 1923, the last American regiment was withdrawn. The Navy, too, came home, but whereas the Army accepted as inevitable its reduction to skeleton dimensions, the Navy expected to remain strong, at least in ships. For upon the fleet rested the task of preventing the invasion of American shores, regardless of what might happen to Wilson's proposed League of Nations. Wartime personnel, however, had to be trimmed down, and the Navy's contribution during 1919 to the number of discharged servicemen reached more than 400,000.[8]

The withering away of government was no part of the capitalistic credo, but by most American business leaders the inability of the government to govern could be viewed without serious alarm. They had learned during the war what the government could really do when it tried; indeed, many of them as temporary government officials had helped construct and administer the governmental machinery that had brought business to heel. The urgent needs of a wartime economy had left little room for competition; in order to meet what Bernard Baruch called "an absolute demand," the government had fostered instead a maximum of "united action and co-operation." Such a transformation involved, among other things, the organization of hundreds of businesses into well-coordinated national associations, "each responsible in a real sense for its multitude of component companies." This development meant in effect monopoly, but for the duration of the war the government also stood guard with extensive controls over prices and distribution, controls that on the whole worked extremely well. According to John Dewey, "The economists and business men called to the industrial front accomplished more in a few months to demonstrate the practicable possibilities of governmental regulation of private business than professional Socialists had effected in a generation."[9] In general, however, the World War I price-fixing program extended only to important industrial materials and to agricultural commodities, but not to the prices of goods in retail trade.

The wartime experience also taught the business leaders who participated in it the great advantages of combination and cooperation over competition. With the war at an end, all they asked was to continue the system that wartime necessities had fostered, excepting only for the elimination of hampering governmental controls. They had no notion of permitting the temporary interference of government in private business to harden into permanent peacetime practice. They were proud of their business acumen, convinced on principle that free enterprise was the only right rule of conduct, and utterly unwilling to surrender longer the power they believed to be rightfully theirs. The correct procedure would be for the government to abandon all limitations on business freedom, and to leave business leaders strictly to their own devices. A reconstruction conference of five thousand businessmen, held in Atlantic City in December, 1918, reflected admirably this point of view. In the eyes of the conference, whatever had happened during the war to promote "the socialization of industry" amounted merely to a "perversion of business from its true course." The sooner the new wartime rules and regulations could be swept away, the better. For good measure, the obsolete and irrelevant restraints of the Sherman and Clayton Antitrust Acts should also go, together with "all other checks on free enterprise."[10]

There were a few warning voices, chief among them Bernard Baruch's. As chairman of the powerful War Industries Board, Baruch had been in the best possible position to observe the revolutionary changes in business that the war had wrought. He was willing to admit, as most businessmen were not, that to leave private operators in complete control of the new economic machinery would subject them "to such temptations as many of them will be unable to resist." Unless the government stepped in with regulations far stronger than any known before the war, business leaders could, for example, use their powers to keep production short of current demand, and so force prices ever higher and higher. Baruch wanted no return to outmoded competitive principles. He recommended the retention of a government agency "clothed with the power and charged with the responsibility of standing watch against and preventing abuses." Industry, on its part, was to practice self-restraint, "to help and not to hinder." Perhaps Baruch was already thinking in terms of what later blossomed forth as the National Recovery Administration.[11]

Even if the postwar government had remained strong, which it did not, it could hardly have held on to its wartime supremacy over business. For if business had experienced no "spiritual rebirth" out of the war, neither had government. What nearly everyone seemed to want, long before Harding coined the phrase, was the speediest possible "return to normalcy." Postwar changes in the Cabinet, such as the substitution of Houston for McAdoo as Secretary of the Treasury and Palmer for Gregory as Attorney-General, tended if anything to promote conservatism. In Congress reaction was openly triumphant. In the words of one caustic critic, Congress represented in reality only "the upper class, the possessing class," perhaps only "5% of the people—a vast majority [of Congress] representing a small minority [of the people]." Understandably, therefore, it would "tolerate no modification of the old economic order." Even the President seemed resigned to this situation. In his annual message of December, 1918, he had admitted that no plausible system of "reconstruction" had emerged from the war and that any attempt to put the people "in leading strings" would be sure to fail. He had also hoped for more from the new Industrial Board than it was able to deliver.[12]

The absence of any careful planning for peace, as indicated by the demobilization procedures, was perfectly obvious. It was natural that public interest should center principally on the winning of the war; moreover, the official propagandists were extremely critical of any line of thought that might distract attention from what they called the "war effort." Was it quite patriotic, under the circumstances, even to think or talk about postwar problems? The war had no sooner ended, however, than professional liberals, such as Walter Weyl and William Hard, began to feature the economic readjustments that would have to be made. How were the demobilized servicemen and the discharged war workers to find jobs? The crying need, these publicists believed, was for public works to provide "buffer employment." "If private enterprise cannot supply the work," wrote Hard in December, 1918, then government must do it "through the taxing power." But plans for public expenditures, whether by national, state, or local authorities, were practically nonexistent. President Wilson, in his first message to Congress following the war, advocated public works in principle, but he failed to spell out any national program, and Congress made no effort to translate his words into deeds. Nor did the conference of governors and mayors that the President called to meet in Washington, March 3-5, 1919, with a view to stimulating state and local public works, achieve any important results. The root trouble, of course, was that the plans should have been laid long before. At war's end was too late.[13]

Nor had any govermental agency turned its attention seriously to the critical problem of winding up war contracts. When the United States entered the war in 1917, the general assumption was that the fighting would last much longer than it did—four years was a not unusual estimate. Acting under the joint pressures of patriotism, profits, and governmental insistence, American business had turned enthusiastically to war production. Industrialists found new wartime uses for their products, retooled all or parts of their plants for war necessities, and created some new "war babies" strictly for the purpose of producing war materials. By the time of the armistice American industry was at the peak of production, with every expectation that the wartime boom would continue well into

the future. Then, with a suddenness that few had fore-
seen, the war came to an end, and the cancellation of
orders began. Whereas, only a few months before, government buyers had thought in terms of the goods needed
for a prolonged war, now they apparently assumed that
peace would be eternal and war forever a thing of the
past. Perhaps if the war had lasted longer, as expected,
both the government and business would have given more
consideration to the problems of transition from production for war to production for peace. But as it was, government authorities began at once to cancel war orders,
apparently with no slightest concern for the results on
business. Rumor had it that on November 12, the day
after the signing of the armistice, long-distance commu-
nications from Washington broke down completely under
the weight of the cancellation messages. Within a period
of four weeks producers saw about $2.5 billion worth of
contracts vanish into thin air.[14]

Coincident with the cancellation of war orders came
also the elimination of the various devices by which the
government had controlled business. Price ceilings, so
fundamental to the war economy, began to disappear
within two days after the signing of the armistice. Fuel
regulations, used extensively during the war to keep the
war producers in coal, vanished almost as promptly. The
priority system of allocating materials, possibly the most
powerful of the wartime restraints on business, did not
last out the year. By order of Congress, in December,
1918, the United States Housing Corporation, created
early in the war to provide housing for war workers, discontinued construction on all buildings less than 70 per
cent completed. War offices in Washington, through
some of which while the war lasted American business
had received its directives, folded so suddenly that many

discharged employees, bereft of pay checks, lacked the funds necessary to buy transportation home. To solve this problem for the War Industries Board stenographers, Bernard Baruch put up $45,000 out of his own pocket and received from the delighted girls a deluge of thank-you notes; the "Chief's" generosity had enabled them to spend Christmas with their families.[15]

The suddenness and planlessness with which the government had liquidated its obligations to business can hardly be excused. Both the War Industries Board and the Department of Labor urged the War Department not to cancel contracts without consideration of the effects on the communities concerned, but all such protests were ignored. As a World War II planning board reported twenty-five years later, what the government did after World War I "was laissez faire with a vengeance; the Government created the disturbance in the economic system, then ignored the results." These results were sometimes devastating. Generally speaking, the firms with the fewest government contracts fared best, and the "war babies" fared worst. But all along the line there was trouble as the demands of war disappeared and the demands of peace could only be surmised. Some firms were plunged immediately into bankruptcy or dissolution; others were left to spend months or years in seeking, but not always obtaining, compensation from the government for the cancellations they had suffered; nearly all had to change their plans for the future with a minimum of forethought. From Armistice Day to the middle of 1919 there was a "hesitation period," during which businessmen tried frantically, but not always with immediate success, to re-adjust themselves to peace conditions. The seriousness of this recession should not be underestimated. Production dropped off in all basic industries—iron, steel, copper, chemicals, textiles. Unemployment mounted. What needs explanation is why the downward spiral, so inauspiciously begun, was so quickly arrested and turned into a business boom.[16]

The nation's business leaders took full credit for this happy transformation. Those who had been in government service departed from Washington in almost unseemly haste, so eager were they to return to their customary pursuits. Perhaps some of them thought, as William Hard wrote, "the war is over; let us forget it. Let us make money and have a good time." Whatever their motives, they tackled with right good will the problem of reconversion, and in general mastered it easily. The shortness of American participation in the war had made total conversion to war production unnecessary for most plants. Even in 1918, when about one-fourth of the national product was allocated to war purposes, the manufacture of ordinary civilian goods remained at a high level, much higher proportionately than during World War II. Many factories had devoted only part of their space to war work, and could resume full production for civilian use without serious strain. Others that had supplied such items as uniforms, blankets, and shoes had virtually no reconversion problem at all. Plants that had retooled for the production of arms and ammunition faced the greatest difficulties and, as already noted, some of these "war babies" did not survive. But the greatest anxiety of the business world was not reconversion; it was customer demand. Where were the orders coming from to replace the war orders that the government had canceled?[17]

Surprisingly the new orders soon began to come in. Business was bad during the winter of 1918-1919, but even then the signs of recovery were unmistakable. War curtailments had restricted considerably for the preceding two years the output of automobiles and furniture, both of which registered significant increases before the end of 1918. The demand for nondurable goods, especially civilian clothing and fabrics, grew steadily from February on. There was evidence of new life also in the field of residential construction. By the second quarter of 1919 the upward swing, although somewhat spotty, was marked enough to justify a high degree of optimism, while by the third quarter the volume of demand had increased so much that in some lines more orders had piled up than the factories could fill. By this time the boom was on, with a peak of production 19 per cent higher than during the base year of 1914, higher even than during the last quarter of 1918, when war production had reached its maximum. Furthermore, the gross national product of goods and services for 1919 exceeded that of 1918, $41.8 billion as against $41.6 billion, thus making 1919 the biggest business year, except for 1917, that the nation had so far seen.[18]

Current opinion usually ascribed the boom to "deferred demand," that is, consumers who had been unable to buy what they wanted or needed while the war was on indulged in a compensatory buying spree after the war, and so produced the exaggerated demand in 1919. Present-day economists, however, take a very dim view of this theory. The fallacy, they argue, lies in the fact that there was not any really significant deprivation for Americans during the war, even in durable goods; the war did not last long enough, and the production of civilian goods was not sufficiently curtailed. Moreover, except for automobiles and housing, the people's desires were more moderate then than in the years to come; such household items as electric refrigerators and radios were virtually unknown and unavailable. The government had made some effort during the war to promote "moral restraint" as a curb on civilian buying, but the advertisers had fought all such propaganda with an energetic "anti-thrift" campaign. The better part of wisdom, they insisted, was to buy as usual, and thus keep the producers of consumers' goods in business. Probably the two attitudes about canceled each other out. At any rate, few people had laid by sufficient savings during the war to provide the backlog of purchasing power assumed to exist. Many purchasers of Liberty bonds had had no choice but to buy their quotas on credit, and in payment they had promptly turned over their bonds to the banks. Others used the bonds they bought as if they were money, often to meet such pressing obligations as grocery bills. Wartime wages, in short, were usually spent during the war and not saved up for postwar spending. According to Kuznets' figures, consumer savings "were unusually high in 1919 in relation to income, and expenditures abnormally low." Had there been any spending spree as the result of pent-up demand, current as well as past savings would almost certainly have been involved.[19]

If "deferred demand" did not bring on the business boom of 1919-1920, then what did? Businessmen who were sure that their own superior talents and the virtues of free enterprise had uncovered latent buying power and restored prosperity would have found the answer extremely unpalatable. Actually the key to the situation lay in the continuation of heavy government spending, for despite the wholesale cancellations of war contracts the government for many months after the war was unable to avoid spending with almost wartime prodigality. Part of the spending consisted of loans to European countries, loans which the public generally lumped in with the "war debts," but which were actually "peace debts" designed to promote European recovery. These loans, while they lasted, permitted Europe to continue its wartime practice of purchasing generously in the United States. An additional factor was that the United States Treasury had to borrow a large proportion of the money it was spending. This involved deficit financing and an easy credit policy, with a corresponding shot in the arm to the economy, not fully understood even by economists until many years later. The net result of these forces acting together was a high level of domestic prosperity that led to increased spending, and an unhealthy volume of speculation. When government spending dropped off and reconstruction loans ceased, and when the Treasury began to operate in the black instead of in the red, the postwar boom collapsed.[20]

It is tempting to compare the little boom and collapse of 1919-1920 with the big boom and collapse that came a few years later. Undoubtedly unrestrained free enterprise, as, for example, in the manufacture of automobiles, loomed much larger in the latter period than in the former. But there were conspicuous similarities. The government of the United States may have balanced its budget throughout the 1920's, but many state and local governments did not. Their spending, especially on highways, played a role almost comparable to that of national spending in the preceding years; moreover, heavy private loans to Europe, which the national government encouraged, were about as hazardous and served much the same purpose as the earlier public loans. Above all, there was a failure on the part of the national government in both instances to realize where its easy money policy would lead. In a strictly limited sense, the little boom and collapse of the postwar years may be regarded as a kind of precursor to the big boom and collapse of the 1920's; if you will, a rehearsal for disaster.

Postwar government expenditures on the home front included a number of significant items. Soldiers who were returned to private life each received the sum of $60 in cash and transportation home, in the aggregate a considerable outlay. The cancellation of war orders was not as ruthless as it was usually made to appear, for the government normally allowed each company that had lost a contract a full month's additional production, to be distributed over a longer period of time if the company desired. The shipbuilding program begun during the war was continued unabated for two years after the fighting ceased, with monthly expenditures at or near wartime levels. The persistence of this program was not altogether a matter of planning; so great an undertaking simply could not be discontinued in a short period of time. But it is true also that the new ships were needed to replace war losses, and that the United States government definitely intended to build up a strong merchant marine for postwar purposes. When the armistice was signed, the Emergency Fleet Corporation, which operated under the United States Shipping Board, had delivered only about three million tons of shipping; in the next two years it delivered about six million tons. The railroads, because plans were not ripe for their return to their owners, remained under government operation until March, 1920. Probably the extravagance of the Railroad Administration was less marked than some critics believed, but during the year 1919 it made capital expenditures of $570 million, only $20 million less than in 1918, not to mention the heavy deficit in operating expenses that the government had to make up.[21]

Loans by the United States to European nations after the armistice amounted to well over $3 billion. To a considerable extent this continuation of wartime policy was mere inertia; it was hard to break off a great and well-established program. But there were those who saw the importance to the United States of aiding the hard-hit European economies. Frank A. Vanderlip, for example, had in mind something akin to the Marshall Plan adopted after World War II. "The re-starting of the wheels of industry *everywhere in Europe*," he maintained, "is a prerequisite to security." He foresaw that if Europe should be permitted to disintegrate further, there might be "let loose forces" that would be "more terribly destructive than have been the forces of war." In general, however, Americans had little understanding of the significance to them of the European economic situation, nor did the action of the government in continuing loans rest upon any well-conceived plan. Whatever the forces that led to the continuation of the loans, the money lent did enable the exhausted nations to buy extensively in the United States, and thus to stimulate immeasurably the postwar American boom.[22]

Throughout the war years, and until October, 1919, deficit financing supplied a great proportion of the funds that the Treasury paid out. The peak of government expenditures came actually in December, 1918, and the next highest month was January, 1919. For the last quarter of 1918 the government was spending, in excess of revenue received, at the rate of $20 billion a year. During the first quarter of 1919 this rate of spending declined to $11 billion, during the second quarter to $6 billion, and during the third quarter to $3 billion. Thereafter Treasury receipts began to exceed expenditures, although the effects of deficit spending continued on for some time. The last of the five great bond issues, the Victory Loan of $4.5 billion, did not occur until April, 1919. Like its predecessors, the Victory Loan greatly expanded bank credit by providing a plentiful supply of bonds to be used as collateral for loans, thus creating commercial paper that bankers could in turn rediscount with the Federal Reserve Banks, and so obtain still more money to lend. Furthermore, as long as government borrowing continued, the Federal Reserve policy was definitely to keep down the rediscount rate, and so to insure easy credit. Probably, also, government borrowing drew into circulation funds which might otherwise have remained idle. Certain it is that, as long as the boom continued, the totals of bank loans and of money in circulation rose steadily. Gold accumulations, due to heavy deposits made during the war in payment for goods exported, had risen from $18.5 billion before the war to $30 billion, thus insuring that the legal minimum of 40 per cent backing in gold for Federal Reserve Bank issues could easily be met.[23]

Easy credit alone, as later events were to prove, could not bring on a business boom. There must also be an adequate demand. And the demand existed. Automobiles and houses, clothing and furniture, as already noted, supplied some of the demand, but hardly enough to create a boom. Foreign purchases were more important, for if the devastated nations of Europe no longer needed war goods, they needed everything else, most especially cotton and food for their cold and hungry masses. To help meet their credit needs, Congress created a new American Relief Administration, with Herbert Hoover at its head, and authorized it to sell relief supplies to the war-torn countries on credit, a privilege later extended also to the United States Grain Administration. Great as was the foreign demand for American goods during wartime, it became still greater in 1919. Exports from the United States increased from a total of $3.2 billion in the first ten months of 1918 to $4.26 billion in the first ten months of 1919. During the same period exports to Germany, nonexistent in 1918, rose to $54.2 million. Not all of these purchases were paid for by government loans. There was some resumption of normal sales by Europe to the United States, and even if, according to *The Nation,* American bankers were "losing opportunities for legitimate extension of American credit abroad," many American business firms sold freely on credit to foreign purchasers, locomotives and rolling stock, for example, to replace the heavy losses suffered during the war. According to careful estimates, the total amount of private credit extended by American producers to European purchasers amounted in 1919 to $1.7 billion, and in 1920 to $2.7 billion.[24]

The creation of a boom requires something more than the supplying of goods to meet legitimate needs; the essential final ingredient is speculation. In the boom of 1919-1920 the greatest speculative influence took the odd form of over-accumulation of inventories. The fear of shortages during the war had become a kind of obsession, although there was little basis for it in fact. After the war certain shortages did exist, for example in clothing and house furnishings, and to make sure of deliveries buyers sometimes placed the same orders with several firms, hoping that at least one firm would be able to make good. The steady procession of strikes in 1919 also had its effect; with labor troubles so rife, dealers deemed it expedient to keep on hand plentiful supplies of all sorts of goods. Likewise, the danger of revived competition from the war-wrecked factories of Europe seemed slight.

Deceived by these circumstances, and encouraged by the powerful volume of foreign demand, manufacturers not only produced goods in maximum amounts, but they also built new plants to enable them to produce still more goods. By 1920 the annual increase in new investment had reached $3 billion, more than during any war year, and more than in any year between the two wars. Meantime the value of piled-up inventories had grown during 1919 by $6 billion, a figure twice as great as that of any year in the following decade, and nearly four times as great as in all but one of them, 1923. Rising prices accelerated the process as buyers sought to lay in plentiful supplies at low figures for sale later at higher figures. But "forward-buying" of consumers' goods was not the only speculative influence. City and country real estate also began to appreciate fantastically in value, with heavy turnovers and long profits for dealers. And the stock market, too, responded to the new influences. The average number of shares traded each month on the New York Stock Exchange in 1914 was 19.4 million. By 1918, the last year of the war, it was down to 12 million. But by 1919 it was up to more than 26 million, with call money bringing 7 per cent in June, 18 per cent in July, and 30 per cent in November. The speculation craze had caught hold.[25]

While many contemporary observers assumed that the high postwar prices resulted from customer competition for an inadequate supply of goods, the truth, as we have seen, was quite different. Actually, the frantic efforts of dealers to pile up excess inventories was the principal culprit. There was in reality no serious shortage of goods; the trouble was that dealers who had overordered had to have correspondingly higher prices to operate at a profit. The postwar demand for housing and for automobiles might have contributed something toward price inflation, and the absence of price controls was undoubtedly a factor. But the soaring prices of 1919-1920 were in the main speculative. During the war price levels had risen from 10 to 15 per cent each year, and in early 1919 they had started to drop. But beginning in April, 1919, they rose steadily until by June, 1920, they had passed their wartime peak by 25 per cent, with wholesale prices at about two and one-half their prewar levels.

Naturally the sudden rise in prices provoked angry outcries from the public, for wage and salary increases had not kept pace. Businessmen insisted that the fault could not possibly be theirs. The *Journal of Commerce and Commercial Bulletin* felt obliged to brand as a fallacy the "notion that large profits earned . . . by corporations or business enterprise result in higher prices and hardship to the workers." However this might be, the high cost of living, usually abbreviated to "h.c.l.," became for the masses a principal subject of conversation. Probably the people, as usual, bought all they could afford to buy, but dealers with overstocked shelves and warehouses were convinced that their customers were staging a buyers' strike in order to drive prices down. The government took a hand by putting on the market at cut-rate prices about $2 billion worth of surplus war supplies, including such items as clothing and canned goods. Sold first to industrial buyers, these commodities reached the public mainly through the well-known "Army and Navy" stores, but the volume of such sales was too small to affect the price structure as a whole. Governmental restraints, national, state, and local, were also attempted, especially to curb rising rents, but without wartime compulsion all such efforts proved to be singularly ineffective.[26]

The speculative fever of 1919-1920 lasted only while prices continued to rise; indeed, it could not long survive even a decline in the rate of acceleration. By midsummer, 1920, postwar prices reached their highest peak, and turned sharply downward. Before the decline was arrested in 1922 wholesale prices had fallen by a total of 45 per cent, sometimes at the rate of 3 per cent per month, a more severe slump in a shorter period of time than occurred after either the panic of 1873 or that of 1929. The corresponding rise in retail prices had been less spectacular, and the fall during the depression months was only about 12 or 13 per cent. These figures represent averages; there were multitudinous variations. "How cheerful it is," carped one critic, "to see a $4 pair of shoes marked down from $20 to $17.98." Or, as *Life* took pains to note, "The High Prices are climbing down but they are proceeding slowly, as if afraid they might hurt themselves." That was at the beginning of the price decline; later on the shoe customer could buy a $4 pair of shoes for $4. Meantime, as dealers who were caught with more goods in stock than they could sell canceled orders right and left, industrial production fell off, the gross national product dropped from $40.1 billion in 1920 to $37.6 billion in 1921, unemployment mounted to about 4,750,-000, and bankruptcies multiplied.[27]

Since the downward turn of prices had coincided closely with government discontinuance after May 31, 1920, of the $2.26-per-bushel price support on wheat, the general assumption was that the removal of the agricultural subsidy was what had triggered the collapse. But other forces than the blow to wheat no doubt bore a far greater responsibility for bringing the boom to an end. Foremost among them was the fact that government spending had begun to taper off and deficit financing had come to an end. During the first two quarters of 1920 Treasury receipts exceeded Treasury expenditures by $831 million, in contrast with the huge deficits piled up during the preceding years. The solvent condition of the

Treasury reflected less spending by the government at home, less lending to foreign governments, and higher tax receipts, in part as a result of increases in rates imposed by the lame-duck Democratic Congress in February, 1919. The discontinuance of deficit financing also brought to an end the process of credit inflation on which the boom had fed; the familiar cycle of expanding bank credit with each new issue of bonds had played out. Instead, the Treasury, by taking in annually more than $1.5 billion above expenditures, was levying a heavy toll on income and purchasing power.[28]

There were many other interesting factors that served to promote deflation. Late in 1919 the Federal Reserve officers decided that the inflation of the currency would have to be checked; otherwise they might face the depletion of their gold reserves below the 40 per cent minimum set by law. They therefore warned bankers to tighten up on collections, and for good measure they raised rediscount rates, from 4.75 per cent at the end of 1919 to 5.5 per cent in late January, 1920, and to 7 per cent the following June. While this action may have had little effect on the worst speculators, who were notoriously indifferent to high interest rates, it probably did serve as a check on legitimate business. Rediscounts reached a maximum of $2.8 billion in October, 1920, then declined steadily to only $387 million by August, 1922. During the year 1921 the value of Federal Reserve notes in circulation fell by a total of $1 billion. This tightening up of private credit also had a deleterious effect on foreign buying, which was already seriously hit by the declining volume of government loans, the revival of European production, and the increased foreign competition that the United States had to face as more and more shipping became available to transport non-American goods. Dealers engaged in unloading oversized inventories at reduced prices also did their bit toward reducing demand; they had no need to order more goods until their stocks were adequately depleted. Unemployment cut seriously into urban purchases, while low agricultural prices reduced the farmers' ability to buy. Meantime housing construction, much as it was needed, fell off rapidly, stock-market prices began a dizzy descent, and speculation of every sort and kind collapsed. For two full years or more the nation's business was at low ebb.[29]

Under these circumstances, what did business want from government? First and foremost, a drastic reduction in the heavy wartime taxes. The excess profits tax, the surtax on high incomes, and all other such curbs on business incentive must end. Just as "profit in the form of capital investment" increases the wealth of the country, the argument ran, so excessive taxation "takes away the means of increasing the wealth of the country." If the high taxes continued, capital would go on strike, production would shrink, unemployment would grow. Investors would put their money into tax-exempt government securities rather than into new enterprise. It was therefore up to Congress "to unshackle industry, to set free initiative, and to stimulate production" by lowering taxes. If by any chance a reduction of taxes on income and profits should leave the government with inadequate revenue, then why not raise the essential amounts through taxes on gross or retail sales? Former Secretary of the Treasury William G. McAdoo had another suggestion. Taxes were indeed "having an injurious effect on business," he said, and should be reduced by $1 billion annually. Rather than resort to new taxes, however, he would fund the deficit in long-term bonds. But the current Secretary of the Treasury, David F. Houston, while convinced that taxes were too high and ought to be lowered, held that further bond issues were both unnecessary and unwise.[30]

Businessmen also demanded with near unanimity that the government abstain from further lending to European nations and lay plans for the collection of the money already lent. The war debts were in part responsible for the high taxes, and the drain on the Treasury for foreign loans must cease. Early in 1920 Secretary Houston announced that the American government would adhere to the policy of no new loans, but out of deference to Europe's continuing needs the United States would postpone further interest payments for a period of at least three years. Since up to this time European nations had paid their interest only by additional borrowing from the American Treasury, this moratorium gave them no immediate aid, and unless their credit needs could somehow be met, the resulting breakdown in commerce and exchange could become catastrophic, both for them and for the United States. American bankers were hesitant, but great as was the risk of granting credit to Europe, there were those who thought that it might be a greater risk to refuse it. The consensus of opinion in business circles, however, was that the credit to be extended must be private, and not public. According to Herbert Hoover, "The resort to direct loans by the United States Government to foreign governments with the intention of promoting commerce can lead only to vicious ends." Instead, Hoover recommended "the systematic permanent investment of our wealth from surplus production in reproductive enterprise abroad," while the American Bankers Association proposed the creation of a foreign trade financing organization with $100 million capital. Although the credits already extended by American firms to European purchasers were substantial, optimists argued that the United States, "if we set about it in a big organized way," could "place a large volume of our surplus products abroad with perfect safety."[31]

To most of the makers of business opinion, the retreat of the government from the field of foreign loans was only one phase of a general retreat. "The government has no part in private business," one writer insisted, "except to protect the individual against imposition." Nor was the government's responsibility for the protection of the individual to be interpreted too generously. The business world accepted with much gratification the decision of the United States Supreme Court in the United States Steel Corporation case (1920). By a four to three vote, with two judges abstaining, the court refused to order the dissolution of the steel trust, although it was a holding company of formerly competing corporations and controlled half the steel output of the country. Mere size did not matter, the court held, in the absence of proof that the corporation was seeking to destroy its remaining competitors or was conspiring with them to fix prices. This decision pretty well brought to an end the "trust busting" efforts begun long before by Theodore Roosevelt.

Thus encouraged, business did not hesitate to voice its protest against the regulatory efforts of government in general. While existing federal agencies need not be abolished, their membership should be so altered as to give the business world greater representation. Only in exceptional cases should governmental limitations on business be permitted. One such exception was the railroads. Since these corporations "had lived off their final ounce of fat when the government took them over" in 1917, they were in no position to carry on unaided after March 1, 1920, the date that the government returned them to their private owners. There was little agreement on what the government should do for the railroads, and the Transportation Act of 1920 was a compromise. But there was the frankest recognition on all sides that the government's responsibilities for them were not yet at an end. Another exception was the United States Shipping Board and its subsidiary, the Merchant Fleet Corporation, whose temporary status Congress defined in the Merchant Marine Act of 1920. Ultimately the government should get out of the shipping business, but that might take time.[32]

While governmental participation in business, and even regulation beyond the barest minimum, found little favor with the business world, government aid to business was quite another matter. It was up to the government, for example, to guarantee profits for the hard-pressed railroads, and as long as necessary to subsidize in some fashion the newly created merchant marine. The government might also have to draw on its resources to open the way for commercial aviation. The tariff, too, should be so adjusted as to stimulate home industry and at the same time to make possible the reduction of other and more disagreeable forms of taxation; on occasion, tariff rates might even be used to promote a more generous welcome in foreign countries for American exports. Manufacturing concerns deserved every possible encouragement. According to Charles M. Schwab of United States Steel, "every pound of raw material we ship out of the country is a potential loss of employment." It was up to the American nation as a well-developed country to export its surplus in the form of finished products, and to receive in return the raw materials it needed. Whatever the government could do to promote this worthy end was well worth the doing. Among other things, it should keep down shipping charges, and permit free, or nearly free, passage for American ships through the Panama Canal.

Oil interests urged that the government give them diplomatic backing in their quest of foreign oil fields. Above all else, the government should aid business in the disciplining of labor. Labor should somehow be forced to give up "the doctrine of fixing wages artificially by some indefinite standard that can never be settled." With labor, as with commodities, the law of supply and demand should be allowed to operate without interference.[33]

In addition to all these things, business wanted from government frugality, efficiency, and cooperation. Businessmen agreed that the time had come for the government to establish a Budget Bureau through which to plan its expenditures in a systematic manner. With some reluctance Congress, which doted on the old hit-and-miss system, approved in 1920 a measure to create such an organization. But the Republican majority could not resist the temptation to take a slap at Wilson by making the Comptroller-General removable only by a concurrent majority of Congress. To Wilson this restriction seemed both unwise and unconstitutional, so he vetoed the bill. Later Harding accepted it in slightly modified form; the Comptroller-General might be removed by a joint resolution, which required the President's signature, rather than by a concurrent resolution, which did not. In reality businessmen were not too optimistic about what the Budget Bureau could do; it was idle to expect much by way of frugality and efficiency from government, and a certain amount of incompetence would have to be tolerated. More important was the idea of full cooperation between government and business, it being well understood all the while that business was the senior and government the junior partner. The real success of the nation, businessmen knew, depended on the leadership they, and they alone, were able to furnish. Government must never get in the way of business; it might aid business all it could, but it must never arrogate to itself any right to control. The nation's strength depended on business.[34]

Considering that business held government in relatively low esteem, it did not seem unreasonable to keep the Presidency where Wilson's illness had landed it—in virtual impotence. Politicians rather than businessmen brought about the nomination of the incompetent Harding, but the downgrading of government that this action implied entirely satisfied the business world. Harding's campaign chest did not lack for business contributions; with such a man in office business could expect the maximum amount of cooperation from government, and no presumptions of leadership. Harding's selection of Andrew W. Mellon, the aluminum king, to be his Secretary of the Treasury clinched the matter. Business would be in the driver's seat; Mellon was to be, as a later observer noted, the only Secretary of the Treasury under whom three different Presidents served. For a decade the status of business as senior partner in the affairs of state was not to be seriously questioned. Congress came to acquire a disagreeable quota of "sons of the wild jackass," as Senator Moses called all Progressives, but they were only a conspicuous minority; in general the majority in Congress had no desire to challenge business control.

Under business leadership prosperity was destined soon to return; from 1923 to 1929 it reached a brilliant crescendo. The business formula for recovery had worked; business leadership had been vindicated. The great trouble was that the same formula that created the boom also created the depression. It is not surprising, therefore, that during the 1930's certain conspicuous alterations occurred in the pattern of relationship between government and business.[35]

The
Role of
Labor

The loyalty of labor to the American cause during the First World War was as marked as the loyalty of the public in general; it would be impossible to separate the two, and say "This was the attitude of labor," and "This was the attitude of the public." Well before the United States entered the war, on March 12, 1917, a conference called by the Executive Council of the American Federation of Labor, in which the railroad brotherhoods also participated, pledged labor "to defend, safeguard and preserve the Republic . . . against its enemies whosoever they may be." In this same document, however, the labor representatives called upon the government to cooperate with organized labor to the end that the "services in government factories and private establishments, in transportation agencies, all should conform to trade union standards." Fully conscious of the role that labor would have to play in the winning of the war, President Wilson named Samuel Gompers to the important Advisory Commission, as a kind of "ambassador for labor," and accepted a formula that was to last for the duration. On the one hand, the government would recognize the "principle of unionization" and would seek to protect the workers from "disastrous changes in the price level"; on the other, labor agreed not to embarrass the government by "basic strikes."[1]

Inevitably the war produced many problems for labor, but the bargain labor made with the government was reasonably well kept. The government in building cantonments, for example, accepted labor standards as its own, and in setting up the powerful War Labor Board gave labor equal representation with employers. Samuel Gompers thoroughly enjoyed his participation in what he regarded as "a crusade inspired by concern for the higher welfare of humanity and glorifying the spirit of service," and he took especial satisfaction in working toward these ends with his former adversaries. Labor difficulties during the war there were, some of them involving strikes and work stoppages, but the cost-plus system in government contracts made labor-employer agreements relatively easy, and government pressure did the rest.[2]

Labor, on the whole, profited greatly from the war. Wages rose even more rapidly than prices, so that in terms of purchasing power, or "real wages," the worker as the war ended was getting a better return for his labor than he had received before the war. The menace of unemployment seemed likewise to have disappeared. Membership in trade unions had almost doubled. Union treasuries were full, and labor leaders, counting on the liberal provisions of the Clayton Act of 1914, felt a reasonable security in their right to bargain collectively, and to strike if need be without fear of hampering injunctions.[3]

Labor confidence got its first rude shock with the brief recession that followed the signing of the armistice; the status of war workers and of peace workers, it soon appeared, could be vastly different. During the war period every effort had been made to tap new sources of labor supply. With so many men in service, and with European immigration at a standstill, employment agents had induced Negroes and poor whites to leave the South in great numbers for jobs in the northern cities. Mexicans, Puerto Ricans, and Filipinos were likewise in great demand. More and more women had gone to work outside the home, replacing men not only in white-collar jobs but also in such unskilled activities as freight handling. The United States Employment Service of the Department of Labor, formerly interested mainly in securing jobs for immigrants, had organized local boards in nearly every community, and had funneled off the available labor supply to the points of greatest need. Altogether, civilian employment figures by the time of Armistice Day had reached about forty million persons, of whom nearly one-fourth were engaged in some kind of war work.

With wages at unheard of figures, most workers assumed, quite mistakenly as events proved, that their newly found prosperity would last on indefinitely. Then, immediately after Armistice Day, the cancellation of war contracts touched off a cycle of wholesale dismissals. In the midst of a hard winter, thousands of men who had no resources except the daily wages they earned found themselves without jobs. They were soon joined by thousands of ex-servicemen in search of employment, and by a smaller, but still considerable, number of former federal employees, particularly those discharged by the rapidly evaporating war boards. Some of the women who lost their jobs could return to their domestic duties, and some of the rural workers who had come to the cities could return to the farm. But great numbers of war workers found themselves stranded in a strange environment, and with little prospect of re-employment. By February, 1919, an estimated 3 million workers were out of jobs.[4]

The government did little to help this unfortunate situation. At this juncture the United States Employment Service could have been of inestimable assistance, but Congress, in its eagerness to turn its back on war developments as rapidly as possible, chose January, 1919, as the time to curtail the appropriations for this agency by some 80 per cent, and thus to hamper its activities when they were never more greatly needed. Wilson, however, did call a conference in Washington of governors and mayors to discuss the problem of unemployment, but the sentiment of the gathering was probably well expressed by Governor Calvin Coolidge of Massachusetts, whose verdict on the returned veterans was that "more than 90 per cent" of them were able to "take care of themselves." The President also urged Congress to institute a public-works program, including reclamation projects, but the economy-minded Republican majority refused to follow his advice. When in the summer of 1919 business began to take on a new lease of life, unemployment declined, but it by no means disappeared.[5]

There were other disturbing considerations. Among them was the thoroughgoing inflation of the price structure that had followed the war. The rise in prices as an inevitable accompaniment of the war was one thing, but their continuing rise after the return of peace was quite another. Prices had begun to climb in 1914 with the outbreak of the war in Europe, and by 1917 when the United States entered the war they were about 70 per cent above the averages of 1913, the last full year of peace. The trouble was that after Armistice Day, with government controls relaxed and deficit financing still in operation, the upward trend persisted. During 1918 the average of prices had risen to approximately 100 per cent over prewar figures, while during 1919 they rose by another 24 per cent. It might be possible to prove statistically that wages had risen correspondingly, but, whatever the averages might show, prices for many workers had far outrun wage increases, and the problem of making ends meet had become extremely precarious. As *Life* commented wryly, "When we receive one of those bulletins showing that foods haven't increased in price, we realize that you can prove anything with figures."[6]

Moreover, the attitude of employers was far from reassuring. Their rejoicing over the demise of the War Labor Board, which for the duration had defended the rights of labor, was open and unashamed. They seemed to regard the reappearance of "a convenient margin of unemployment" as a blessing rather than a curse. Mr. Gompers, said one of their spokesmen, might as well forget the Clayton Act, for labor was a commodity after all. Peace meant a glutted labor market, and with the law of supply and demand back on the throne, labor would have to accept lower wages whether it wanted to or not. Also, the time had come to halt the process of unionization, which had profited altogether too much from government favoritism during the war. Employers should at last feel free to run their businesses without the handicap of outside interference.[7]

Was labor to lose all the gains it had made during the war? Not if it could help it. Fighting a war on the slogan "to make the world safe for democracy" had had some unanticipated results. Why should employers not understand that "their day of absolutism in industry is

gone, the same as absolutism in government is gone."
"What shall it profit a man if he gain democracy for the
whole world, and lose his own at home?" Why should
the sound doctrine "that every individual had the right
to regular and continuous employment at a wage sufficient for the maintenance of proper living conditions" be
so coldly received in business circles? Sensing the
changed atmosphere, Mr. Gompers reluctantly broke off
his pleasant cooperation with the capitalists, and re-
sumed his time-honored role as labor leader. But the
armies of labor he sought to command were no longer so
content with his methods. New conditions, some of the
younger and more radical leaders insisted, called for
fundamental changes in the pattern of labor organization.
The rapid technical advances of the war years had made
possible in many industries the use of much unskilled or
semi-skilled labor, not classifiable by trades or crafts. Why
should these workers not be organized into all-embracing
industry-wide unions? To Gompers and his conservative
associates, firm disciples of the trade-union principle, this
proposal was far too revolutionary to be tenable. But the
fact remained that the American Federation of Labor
accounted for only 4 or 5 million workers, perhaps not
more than one-eighth of the total American labor force.
Did not democracy require that the other seven-eighths
also have a voice?[8]

There was considerable disagreement, also, as to the
political role that labor should play. Why should American workers forever adhere to the Gompers policy of
"voluntarism," with no defenses except economic pressure
and the pitting of the older parties against each other in
quest of minor favors? What help could labor expect
from either the Democrats or the Republicans, "rival
lackeys to the great monopolies"? Why should American

workers not follow the example of British labor, to say nothing of the Soviets, and form a party of its own? "If labor doesn't organize politically," one disillusioned worker observed, "it ought to be enslaved—and probably will be." But against such radical views Gompers and the old guard held the line with firm consistency. At the meeting of the American Federation of Labor in Atlantic City, June, 1919, Gompers was re-elected with only one dissenting vote, and his policies were upheld, but the existence of a strong undercurrent of discontent was too obvious to be overlooked. Predictions were rife that revolutionary changes in policy only awaited Gompers' death or resignation.[9]

Indeed, railroad labor, in its enthusiastic support of the so-called "Plumb plan" for the reorganization of the railroads, seemed unwilling to wait even that long. This plan was drawn by Glenn R. Plumb, an attorney for the railroad brotherhoods, and was officially presented to the government and the public in 1919 as railroad labor's solution for the railroad problem. The plan revealed, first of all, that the brotherhoods were "in no mood to brook the return" of the railroads to private control; instead, they proposed that the government should float 4 per cent bonds from the proceeds of which to purchase all the railroads of the nation at prices ultimately to be determined by the courts. Operation of the railroads as one united system was to be vested in a corporation owned by the government, but controlled by a fifteen-member board of directors, one-third to be appointed by the President to represent the public, one-third to be elected by the operating officials, and one-third by the classified employees. Surplus earnings after expenses were to be divided equally between the government and the employees, with automatic reductions in rates whenever the employees' share of the surplus should exceed 5 per cent of the gross oper-ating expenses. Railroad rates would continue to be supervised by the Interstate Commerce Commission, and the customary rights and privileges of labor were to be duly safeguarded.

Naturally this radical proposal met with a barrage of opposition. The New York *World* denounced it as "a new form of class industry in which the public provides the capital and the workers take the profits." Such a pro-gram might well precede, as some of its proponents no doubt intended, "a drive for the democratization or na-tionalization of all basic industries such as mines, steel mills, packing industries and other enterprises of a na-tional character." It was socialism, or worse, and should be defeated at all costs. Defeated it was, with Gompers and other labor conservatives joining the opposition, and by the Transportation Act of 1920 the railroads were returned to their private owners. But the fear of the radical program inherent in the Plumb plan disturbed conservatives for a long, long time, and was to bear fruit in the ruthless suppression of the Railroad Shopmen's strike of 1922.[10]

As a matter of fact, the year 1919 was the worst year for industrial strife that the United States had ever known. It would be difficult even to list all the strikes that occurred in the nation during that year. According to one computation, the total reached 2,665, and the number of employees involved, 4,160,348. Strikes or lockouts directly affecting the state of New York alone numbered 608 during the first quarter of the year. The first of three strikes by New York's 16,000 harbor work-ers began on January 9, and ultimately idled 50,000 long-shoremen as well. Later in the month 35,000 dress and waist makers went out. In May the ladies' cloak and suit makers struck; in July, the cigar makers; in August, the Brooklyn surface, elevated, and subway workers; in September, the pressmen; and so on throughout the year. The demands of the strikers varied, but they included such items as higher pay, a shorter workday or week, regular wages instead of piecework pay, and recognition of the union. In the settlement of the New York strikes and of those staged elsewhere in the country there was a general tendency to yield a little to labor, especially in view of the still mounting cost of living.[11]

The numerous lesser, and somewhat local, disturbances, however, were almost overlooked in the tumult caused by a few great strikes of nation-wide import. The first of these was the general strike that gripped the city of Seattle for five days early in February, 1919. In this instance the strike was local enough, and at no time was it characterized by violence, but the whole country was alarmed at its revolutionary implications. Seattle was a strongly unionized city, and the Central Labor Council had welcomed the opportunity to show its power by calling a general strike in sympathy with a metal workers' strike in the shipyards. As a result, the merits of the original demands were soon lost sight of in the far more fundamental issue of who really governed Seattle, the committee that directed the strike, or the civilian authorities headed by the somewhat flamboyant mayor, Ole Hanson. For a time, in spite of Hanson's violent threats, the strike committee was in actual control of the city. It showed good judgment in keeping the streets lighted at night, in maintaining milk dispensaries for families with children, and in permitting such necessary services as hospital laundry wagons to operate. Actually the city was more orderly than under normal conditions. But the weight of public opinion, including outside labor leaders, coupled with the growing uneasiness of some of the men on strike, soon induced the strike committee to call a halt to the proceedings, leaving the metal workers to continue their struggle alone.[12]

Almost as upsetting to conservative minds as the idea of a general strike was the idea of a police strike. Indeed, the very thought of policemen's unions seemed to many Americans incompatible with the obligations of law-enforcement officers. But the existence of such unions in England was well known, and early in August, 1919, news came that police strikes had broken out in London and Liverpool. In many American cities the economic plight of the police forces was so desperate, thanks to the persistence of prewar wage scales, that the possibility of gains through unionization made a strong appeal. In Boston, for example, where a policeman's pay could be as low as $1100 a year, a thirteen-year-old organization of policemen, known as the Boston Social Club, reorganized as a union and sought affiliation with the American Federation of Labor. This action was strongly denounced by Boston Police Commissioner Edwin U. Curtis, who pointedly forbade his men to become members of a labor union. In spite of Curtis's stand, the A. F. of L. charter was granted and on August 15 was officially accepted. Thereupon the commissioner charged eight officials of the club with insubordination, and ordered that they be disciplined.

At this juncture, the mayor of Boston, Andrew Peters, stepped into the situation by appointing a Citizens' Committee of Thirty-four to seek a compromise settlement. The committee's report proposed that the policemen be permitted to retain their union, but that they give up affiliation with the A. F. of L.; also that after due investigation there be an adjustment of wages and working conditions, and that no one be penalized for his short-lived A. F. of L. connection. This plan of settlement apparently satisfied the policemen, but the police commissioner peremptorily rejected it and suspended nineteen of the men who had been most active in the movement for organization. In answer, the police force held a mass meeting and voted 1,134 to 2 in favor of a strike.[13]

On September 9, at 5:45 p.m., about 70 per cent of the Boston policemen abandoned their posts, leaving the city in an uproar. Pranksters accounted for most of the trouble, but some store windows were broken in, and thefts did occur. When Police Commissioner Curtis, in spite of a force of volunteers including a number of Harvard students, proved unable to handle the problem, Mayor Peters himself took over, and, as was his legal right, called out the Boston companies of state troops. This action proved sufficient to restore order, although the strike was not yet broken. Finally on the third day of the strike, with the city quieting down and the end in sight, Governor Calvin Coolidge, whose previous inaction Mayor Peters, a Democrat, had openly criticized, announced that the governor was rightfully in command, and called out additional state troops from outside Boston. Coolidge also asked the Secretary of War for federal troops in case a general strike should occur, and on the fourth day of the strike, with its failure clearly indicated, proclaimed that none of the men who had deserted their posts would ever be taken back. This was also the stand of the police commissioner, who began to recruit a new force. When Samuel Gompers urged Coolidge to help the men get their jobs back, the governor, in denying the request, wired back: "There is no right to strike against the public safety by anybody, anytime, anywhere." Actually Coolidge's part in ending the strike had been insignificant, but this statement won him the congratulations of President Wilson, and opened for him the road to the Vice-Presidency and the Presidency.[14]

The Boston police strike was barely settled when, on September 22, 1919, a great strike began in the all-important steel industry. The grievances of the steelworkers were genuine. For more than one-third of the men so employed the workday was twelve hours, and the workweek, seven days. Once in two weeks the men on the blast furnaces were obliged to work an eighteen- or twenty-four-hour shift. Some steel employees worked ten-hour days, but relatively few enjoyed the eight-hour day and forty-eight-hour week, then customary in most American industries. Wages, except for highly skilled employees, were low, the work was incredibly hard, and the risk to life and limb was great. Indeed, native American labor was comparatively rare in the steel mills. Most of the men so employed were immigrants from southern or eastern Europe, and many of them were unable to speak the English language. Their abject poverty, and their ignorance of American customs and political rights, made their exploitation easy. Sometimes they were herded together in unsightly and unsanitary villages where the governing authorities were completely controlled by the steel operators. In such places freedom of speech and the right of free assembly were severely limited, and such undesired visitors as labor organizers quickly ran afoul of the law.[15]

Earlier strikes in the steel mills, such as had occurred in 1901 and 1909, had resulted in a complete victory for the open shop and discriminations against union men, but during the First World War union men were protected from dismissal by the War Labor Board. Thus the unionization of steel could again be attempted. The trade-union system, however, was particularly unfortunate in this instance because no less than twenty-four different unions claimed jurisdiction over one aspect or another of the steelworkers' activities. Somehow unity of action had to be achieved. Finally, in August, 1918, representatives of each of the interested unions agreed to form a National Committee for the Organizing of the Iron and Steel Industry which would first sign up recruits, and then later on divide them among the separate trade unions in accordance with their various crafts. The author of this idea was William Z. Foster, who became secretary of the organizing committee and the leading spirit in its work. Foster, an ex-syndicalist and not yet a Communist, was a strong believer in industrial unionism, but proposed the plan of a joint campaign as the best thing to do under the circumstances. He was a man of driving energy who had come up the hard way, and who knew from bitter experience the problems of the ordinary laborer. His record to date, according to his own summary, included "three years as sailor on square-rigged sailing ships, three years in chemical industry, three years as a homesteader in Oregon, ten years as railroad worker; various terms of employment in building, mining, lumber and farming."[16]

Under Foster's able direction, and with funds contributed by the various cooperating unions, organizers began work in the western steel plants around Chicago, then moved eastward through Indiana and Ohio to the great industrial area around Pittsburgh. The initial drive was enormously successful; organizers found the men eager to sign up. Impressed by what was going on, the United States Steel Corporation and the Bethlehem Steel Company both announced in October, 1918, their acceptance of the basic eight-hour day. But this concession did not mean that the steel manufacturers were content with the progress of unionization. They made every effort to hamper the work of the organizers, and when the special wartime protection of the War Labor Board to union labor ceased, they began wholesale discharges of union men.

Efforts to secure a conference between the unions and the manufacturers proved hopeless. In May, 1919, Judge Elbert H. Gary, Chairman of the Board of United States Steel, told the president of the Amalgamated Association of Iron, Steel and Tin workers that the steel corporation did not "confer, negotiate with or combat labor unions as such." Overtures for a conference from the National Organizing Committee were simply ignored. On July 20 representatives of the twenty-four cooperating unions voted 22 to 2 in favor of circulating a strike ballot. The principal issues were the right of collective bargaining, reinstatement with lost pay for the men discharged because of union activities, the eight-hour day and the six-day week, an end to the twenty-four-hour shift, the check-off and seniority, and a living wage. But Gary persisted in his refusal to consider a conference, and this stand, together with an intensification of repressive measures against unionism, led to the decision in favor of a strike, to begin September 22, 1919.[17]

No doubt the steel corporation welcomed the test of strength that was to follow. Its power was tremendous, and the chance of liquidating the gains made by the unions during the war period seemed good. With the strike date set, President Wilson sought to intervene by asking postponement until a National Industrial Conference he had called should report. But the union leaders would not call off the strike unless the men discharged for union activities should be reinstated, and Judge Gary remained firm in his refusal to treat with union representatives. As a matter of fact the President's Conference, when it met in October, could find no common ground on which the representatives of the public, labor, and capital, of which it was composed, could stand. And so the men went out, according to the National Organizing Committee 343,100 of them, enough to affect nearly every mill in nearly every steel-producing region. Two days later they were joined by numerous employees of the Bethlehem Steel Company, and by the end of September 365,600 men were out.[18]

The strike that followed was long and violent, but almost from the beginning the advantage lay with the employers. Not all the men went out, and with the aid of many new recruits, including Negroes from the South, the production of steel in limited quantities continued. Company agents artfully spread dissension among the workers, and local governmental agencies were generally unfriendly to them. The press made much of William Z. Foster's earlier record of radicalism, and in many other ways used its influence to discredit the strike. The governor of Indiana asked for, and obtained, federal troops to police the city of Gary, and the troops were used to limit picketing. Finally the financial resources of the men began to run out, and they drifted back to work. On January 8, 1920, the National Organizing Committee officially declared the strike at an end. Probably, however, it had not been altogether in vain. The eight-hour day was soon generally instituted, and public understanding of the steelworkers' case began to grow. Ultimately the Interchurch World Movement's *Report on the Steel Strike of 1919* revealed clearly the abuses from which the workers had suffered, and more or less shamed the employers into reforms. But the open shop in the steel industry continued.[19]

Close on the heels of the steel strike came the walkout, November 1, 1919, of approximately 450,000 miners of bituminous coal. The coal industry had benefited from the war hardly less than steel, for the use of soft coal to produce energy was far more common then than later. It has been estimated that 69.5 per cent of the nation's mechanical energy was derived during the First World War from bituminous coal. Coal, rather than oil, furnished practically all the power for railroads and for shipping, while the use of such substitutes as gasoline, natural gas, and hydroelectric power had only just begun to be important. Subsequently, improved methods of using less coal to obtain the same results also cut down on the demand, but during the war the supply of soft coal was of fundamental importance to the national economy.

Fully cognizant of this fact, the Fuel Administration in October, 1917, negotiated an agreement with mine operators and the United Mine Workers of America designed to insure an uninterrupted supply of coal for the duration of the war. The Washington Agreement, as it was usually called, granted substantial wage increases, but also carried a pledge that the miners would not go on strike while the war lasted. To enforce this clause the operators were authorized to collect from each miner who violated the agreement a fine of one dollar for each day he was out on strike, the amount of the fine to be automatically deducted from his pay. The date set for the Washington contract to become effective was April 1, 1918, and it was to continue in force for two years thereafter, unless the war should end sooner. Under this agreement the mines were kept open throughout the war, and thanks to continuous employment the miners made good wages. But the wage rate, actually negotiated in 1917, did not change during the whole course of the war in spite of the upward trend of prices. This was the more extraordinary in view of the fact that the Fuel Administration had agreed in October, 1918, to a dollar a day increase in the pay of the anthracite coal miners.[20]

After Armistice Day, and particularly after the disbandment of the Fuel Administration on April 1, 1919, the bituminous coal miners began to clamor for a new wage scale. The Washington Agreement, many of them maintained, had ended with the armistice, even if the nation was still technically at war. Furthermore, wartime restraints on the operators had been removed, and the Fuel Administration itself had disappeared. Why, then, should there not be a new contract with a new wage scale? Unrest in the Illinois area resulted in an "insurgent" strike of at least 25,000 miners during August, 1919, which the acting president of the United Mine Workers, John L. Lewis, and his lieutenants did their best to suppress, even going to the length of revoking the charters of twenty-four locals. Possibly Lewis's strategy was merely to insist on solidarity of action among the miners, or possibly he at first underestimated the depth of the miners' discontent. Whatever his motives, he reversed his stand at a convention held in September, 1919, and came out for the termination of the Washington Agreement, the elimination of the contract clause, and a strike if these terms were not accepted. To these demands the convention added a six-hour day and a five-day week, a 60 per cent wage increase, time and one-half for overtime, and double pay for Sundays and holidays. When the operators insisted that the Washington Agreement must run for a full two years, the strike was called for November 1, and on that date both anthracite and bituminous coal miners stayed away from the pits.[21]

Meantime President Wilson had made it clear that if a strike occurred the federal government would stand shoulder to shoulder with the operators. The war, he said, was not yet over, and the Washington Agreement was therefore still in full effect. The strike, he declared, "is not only unjustifiable but is unlawful. The law will be enforced and means found to protect the public interest in any emergency that may arise." The Attorney-General of the United States, A. Mitchell Palmer, not only threatened the miners, but on October 30 he obtained a temporary injunction from Federal Judge Albert B. Anderson, District of Indiana, forbidding the strike and restraining the union officials from doing anything to facilitate it. When the men went out anyway, the court made its temporary injunction permanent, and demanded that the union should cancel its strike order not later than November 11. Thereupon, to the surprise of almost everyone, the officials capitulated. In calling off the strike Lewis said: "The United Mine Workers will obey the mandate of the court. We do so under protest. We are Americans. We cannot fight the government." But the men were not so easily persuaded, and for weeks they refused to return to their jobs. Finally, on December 9, the Fuel Administration, which the President had revived to meet the emergency, proposed an immediate 14 per cent increase in wages and an arbitration commission, appointed by President Wilson, to decide all further points at issue. This the union accepted, and the men went back to work. Eventually the commission reported in favor of a 27 per cent pay increase, but ignored the other demands of the strikers.[22]

Thus the coal strike had won something for the miners, although probably far less than could have been defended as reasonable. The demand for a 60 per cent increase in pay was by no means as ridiculous as it sounded to a public which had forgotten that the miners had

had no change in rates of pay since 1917. The six-hour day and the five-day week were proposed primarily as a means of spreading the work in a period of growing unemployment. The idea that the war was over for the operators, who were free to raise prices at will, but not for the miners was absurd. Lewis's strategy, however, was probably good. He no doubt obtained for the miners about all that the circumstances would permit, and he held down to a minimum the time they were out of work. His hold on the union, somewhat precarious before, was now greatly strengthened.[23]

The steady procession of strikes, large and small, told on the nerves of the public and built up hostility for the men who staged them. Spearheading the opposition to radicalism, which was sometimes defined to include mere union-laborism, was the American Legion, an organization of veterans, formed in Paris during March, 1919, by a thousand delegates from various units of the A.E.F. Two months later, at St. Louis, Missouri, the Legion held its first convention in the United States, and adopted a constitution which pledged its members "to foster and perpetuate a one hundred per cent Americanism." To many of those who recited these words, the battle "to make the world safe for democracy" was not yet over but needed to be continued at home, and if necessary by the same methods as were used overseas, against all "subversive" elements. Naturally there were American Legion parades on Armistice Day, November 11, 1919, and one such, staged at Centralia, Washington, was destined to have tragic results. As the parade passed the local I.W.W. hall, the Legionnaires, whose action was not unanticipated, rushed the building, only to be met by a stream of gun fire that killed three paraders and wounded two others. Still another Legionnaire was killed by an I.W.W.—himself a veteran—who that night in turn was taken from jail and lynched.[24]

During the war the Industrial Workers of the World, or I.W.W., had been ruthlessly suppressed, in theory because of their disloyalty to the government, but in fact probably no less because of their unorthodox economic views and the way they tried to promote them. Founded in 1905 to further industrial unionism as opposed to trade unionism, they asserted that "the working class and the employing class have nothing in common. There can be no peace so long as hunger and want are found among millions of working people and the few, who make up the employing class, have all the good things of life. Between these two classes a struggle must go on until the workers of the world organize as a class, take possession of the earth and the machinery of production and abolish the wage system." The I.W.W. strength lay mainly among the unskilled workers of the far Northwest, the miners, lumbermen, longshoremen, and migratory laborers for whom no A. F. of L. unions existed. I.W.W. methods, and for that matter the methods of those who opposed them, were apt to be violent, and "criminal syndicalism" laws designed to destroy the order, if possible, were passed by most of the states in which it was strong. During the war wholesale arrests and convictions of I.W.W. leaders occurred, both by state and by national authority. In a great mass trial, held in Chicago during the summer of 1918 before Federal Judge Kenesaw Mountain Landis, an even hundred of the most outstanding I.W.W.'s were convicted of conspiracy to hamper the prosecution of the war, and received prison sentences, some for as long as twenty years.[25]

The sudden removal of the men who had long headed the order left it in the hands of untried and irresponsible leaders whose ineptitude helped destroy it. The Centralia incident was a case in point. Following that episode, the American Legion raised $17,000 to aid the prosecution, and eventually seven of the men who were implicated received prison sentences of from twenty-five to forty years each. In California, where mere membership in any organization that advocated resort to violence was treated as a felony, and in Oregon, Washington, Idaho, Kansas, and Oklahoma, there were innumerable convictions. Early in 1920 it was estimated that no less than 2,000 members of the I.W.W. were in jail. From this time forward the importance of the order steadily diminished until by the end of the decade it was virtually dead.[26]

The attack on the I.W.W. was only a part of the "Red hysteria" that swept over the country in the period immediately following the war. The source of this frenzy could be traced in part to the success of the Bolshevist revolution in Russia, which not only gave the world an example of a proletarian dictatorship in the Union of Soviet Socialist Republics, but also, through the Third International, or Comintern, conspired to reproduce itself in every other country. Founded at Moscow, in March, 1919, the Comintern, always working in close harmony with the Soviet government, began its propaganda for the creation of a strictly proletarian and revolutionary party in every nation. In the United States extremists such as those who had supported the I.W.W. quickly fell in line, and at Chicago, in September, 1919, formed an American Communist party. They were cold, however, to the overtures of a left-wing Socialist faction that tried to join them, so the Socialist extremists founded a Communist Labor party of their own. Many other splinter parties, all proclaiming their earnest proletarianism, appeared, but a semblance of unity was obtained, first with the creation in

June, 1920, of the United Communist party, and then in December, 1921, when Communist organizations as such got into trouble with the law, of the Workers' party.[27]

The danger of revolution in the United States was certainly microscopic, but the activities of the "Reds" caused grave concern. Such violence as occurred in labor disputes was generally attributed to them. And there were other acts of violence that were hardly the work of friends of orderly government. Post-office officials in New York City, for example, on investigating sixteen suspicious packages, April 30, 1919, found that they contained time bombs, designed for the May Day assassination of as many prominent public officials. Investigation brought to light a total of thirty-four such bombs, all of a kind, for delivery to, among others, Justice Oliver Wendell Holmes of the United States Supreme Court, Federal Judge Kenesaw Mountain Landis, Attorney-General A. Mitchell Palmer, Secretary of Labor William B. Wilson, Governor William Cameron Sproul of Pennsylvania, and Mayor John F. Hylan of New York City. A month later, on June 2, 1919, a bomb destroyed the house of Attorney-General Palmer in Washington and killed a man, probably the one who set it; at about the same hour bomb or dynamite explosions did serious damage to the residences of Mayor Harry Lyman Davis of Cleveland, Justice Albert F. Hayden of Roxbury, Massachusetts, and Judge C. C. Nott of New York City. The grand climax came more than a year later, on the morning of September 16, 1920, when a bomb was exploded in Wall Street, opposite the entrance to the J. P. Morgan Company building, killing thirty-eight persons and sending fifty-seven others to hospitals.[28]

The inevitable newspaper publicity attendant upon these outrages fanned public opinion into a fine frenzy. Labor disturbances were charged to the Reds, whether they were responsible or not, and the persecution of individuals and organizations suspected of sympathy with Communism flourished mightily. For some of the "Red-baiting" the American Legion and similar "one hundred per cent American" orders were responsible, but the government itself soon took a hand. A subcommittee of the Senate Judiciary Committee investigated charges of Bolshevist propaganda in the United States, and produced much lurid testimony. Administrative officers went even further. Under the terms of the Immigration Act of 1917, which primarily had imposed the literacy test, anarchists and all others who advocated the overthrow of government by force, or the unlawful destruction of property, were excluded from entry into the United States, while a subsequent act, passed in October, 1918, under the stimulus of war conditions, authorized the Secretary of Labor to deport any such aliens to their homelands. Armed with this authority, Secretary Wilson ruled that membership in the Communist party was sufficient grounds for deportation, and on his order the transport *Buford* sailed December 21, 1919, from New York for Hargo, Finland, with a cargo of 249 Russian radicals whom his agents had rounded up for deportation. Among the passengers on the "Soviet Ark" were some long-time residents of the United States, such as the confessed anarchists Emma Goldman and Alexander Berkman, who had little expectation of a friendly welcome in Russia, and were by no means eager to make the trip back to their "homeland."

What Secretary Wilson had begun, Attorney-General Palmer continued with enthusiasm. On New Year's Day, 1920, agents of the Department of Justice raided Communist headquarters throughout the nation, and hauled off to jail a total of more than six thousand suspects. Ultimately most of those arrested were released for lack of evidence against them, but many who were American citizens had to run the gauntlet of criminal syndicalism laws in the various states, and many who were aliens were deported. The American Civil Liberties Union furnished what defense it could for the accused, but the hysteria was such that convictions could be obtained on the flimsiest of evidence, and sentences of deportation on even less.[29]

One of the most notable episodes of the Red scare was the trial and conviction of two Italian workmen, Nicola Sacco and Bartolomeo Vanzetti, for the murder on April 15, 1920, of the paymaster and his guard of a South Braintree, Massachusetts, shoe factory. The real murderers, whoever they might have been, escaped with $15,000 in cash, which would seem to explain their motive, but the crime was given a political twist when it was charged against Sacco and Vanzetti, two known radicals who were given to intemperate language and had recently organized a mass meeting in protest against Department of Justice brutalities. In spite of the slenderest evidence and plausible alibis furnished by the defendants, the trials, held a year later, resulted in convictions and death sentences. The case was immediately taken up by liberals who resented what was aptly termed "conviction by atmosphere," not evidence, but innumerable investigations and postponements did not prevent the executions, August 23, 1927, at the Charlestown, Massachusetts, state prison.[30]

While the Red hysteria of the postwar years was mainly directed at such extremists as the I.W.W. and the Communists, even the Socialists did not escape. This was due in part, no doubt, to the failure of the public to discriminate clearly between the orderly and evolutionary methods of change advocated by the Socialists and the violent and revolutionary methods that the Communists stood ready to use whenever the time should be ripe. Both Socialists and Communists advocated the governmental ownership and operation of all the agencies of production and distribution as their ultimate objective, but whereas the Socialists were willing to rely upon peaceful propaganda and the ballot box to achieve their ends, the Communists, whatever temporizing they might deem desirable at a given moment, regarded revolution after the Russian pattern as the only possible way to overthrow capitalism. Communist agitators favored trade unions, or better still industrial unions, and even a labor party, as means of organizing the working classes and of promoting antagonism between workers and employers. They preached without ceasing the doctrine of class hatred. They were willing at all times to use such "innocents" as would go along with them part way toward their goal, but they were also ready to classify such collaborators as "counter-revolutionists" or "enemies of the working classes" whenever they balked at direct action. Increasingly the Communist "party line" followed whatever policy the Comintern might lay down, and the good Communist regarded Russia as the source and center of all political wisdom.[31]

The number of Communists in the United States was always small, and the danger from them was never great. Precise figures are not obtainable, but the membership of the Communist party in 1919 has been estimated at about 35,000 and the Communist Labor party, which it soon absorbed, at about 15,000. Even these numbers are probably too large. Besides the actual members there were numerous "fellow travelers," who more or less consistently followed the party line, but the sum total of their activities could by no stretch of the imagination have been a serious danger to the American nation.[32]

The Socialist party, after the secession of the Communists in 1919, had less than 40,000 dues-paying members and was far from militant, but the Red-baiters gave it no quarter. Partly this was due to the antiwar record of such Socialist leaders as Eugene V. Debs, who in September, 1918, had been convicted in federal court of violation of the Espionage Act, and sentenced to ten years' imprisonment. Perhaps Debs himself was not fully aware of the nature of Communism, for he had described Lenin and Trotzky as the "foremost statesmen of the age." Victor L. Berger, editor of the Milwaukee Socialist *Leader,* on charges similar to those drawn against Debs, received a twenty-year sentence, but the Supreme Court set it aside, and in November, 1918, Berger was elected to Congress. The House of Representatives, by a vote of 309 to 1, refused to seat him, and when he was promptly re-elected, refused again. Not until December, 1923, when the Red scare had abated, was he permitted to take his seat.

In New York State a committee headed by Senator Clayton R. Lusk took volumes of testimony, and recommended a series of repressive measures which failed of enactment only because Governor Alfred E. Smith refused to sign them. The New York Assembly, however, listened with approval while its speaker on January 7, 1920, denounced its five Socialist members to their faces; then the Assembly by an overwhelming majority expelled them. This action was publicly condemned by Theodore Roosevelt, Jr., then a member of the Assembly, and by former Governor Charles Evans Hughes. The stand taken by these men was good evidence that the Red hysteria had not engulfed everyone, but the Lusk bills were passed again at the next session of the legislature and were signed by Smith's Republican successor, Nathan L. Miller. Echoes of the New York attitude were common throughout the other states, and sometimes found expression in such requirements as loyalty oaths for teachers and restrictions designed to insure the teaching of American history along traditional lines.[33]

The strikes of 1919, and the Red scare so frequently associated with them, occurred for the most part after the short recession that followed the war, and during the postwar boom. They were thus the accompaniments of prosperity, not adversity. The strikes, indeed, seem to have had very little effect on the generally high level of industrial production, which continued while they were in progress. Nor can it be said that economic motivation was the principal cause of the drive against the Reds. The prolonged period of industrial strife, however, together with the constantly recurring acts of violence, did much to intensify employer antagonism against organized labor. It is not surprising, therefore, that when the index of prosperity turned sharply downward during the summer of 1920, employers redoubled their efforts to discipline labor.[34]

Whatever camouflage they might choose to adopt, most of the employers concerned really wished to destroy the unions as effective instruments for the defense of labor. They were tired of being pushed around, and proposed to use this golden opportunity to deal organized labor a knockout blow. Labor unions, they argued, were trespassing upon the rights of individuals. In opposition to the idea of collective bargaining, employers emphasized the right of each individual to represent himself— the "American plan," they called it. Everyone should have the right to work on whatever terms he and his employer might agree upon, and should be free from any "interference and discrimination" by union spokesmen. What the antiunion employers claimed they wanted was the "open shop," although at the time such a thing as the "closed shop" was virtually nonexistent in the United States. Union leaders were quick to point out that what these extremists really wanted was a shop closed to union members; "the open shop in a great corporation," as someone phrased it, "would be a closed shop against union men, and therefore would not be what it appeared to be." Everyone knew that in plants where even a minor fraction of the working force belonged to unions, union leaders were often able to speak up effectively on behalf of all the employees, union and nonunion alike. This was the kind of impertinence that the antiunion employers sought to avoid. Some of them were willing to go the whole length of the infamous "yellow dog" contract, which required from each employee a signed statement that he was not then a member of a labor union, and would not join one while working for his present employer.[35]

The movement for the open shop or the American plan, whatever it might be called, was no idle fancy, but had back of it such powerful groups as the United States Chamber of Commerce, the National Association of Manufacturers, the National Metal Trades Association, the National Founders Association, and the like. Open shop associations appeared in nearly every sizable city, and ground out quantities of propaganda which newspapers were encouraged to repeat. Some companies, not content with keeping the unions out of their own plants, even tried to discriminate against employers who made use of union labor; an executive of the Bethlehem Steel Corporation, for example, let it be known that fabricated steel from the Bethlehem plants would not be available for builders and contractors operating on a union shop basis. The intensity of the open shop drive, coming at a time when labor was already in trouble, no doubt had much to do with the drop in union membership from the all-time high of about 5 million in 1920 to less than 3.6 million in 1923.[36]

Other factors also contributed to the humbling of labor. The familiar carrot-and-stick policy, which offered company unions and welfare capitalism as substitutes for independent union organization, found many takers. "It is time to stop talking about sharing equally with labor," Schwab had told the Atlantic City Reconstruction Conference of December, 1918, "and to begin doing it!" Some companies seemingly took his advice; at least by such means they hoped to appease labor, and to make it more docile. Shop committees and labor representation would be fine, provided only that they were not contaminated by any outside influences. And in a period of declining employment, employees could hardly be blamed for accepting the proffered favors.[37]

The courts, too, gave little comfort to organized labor. In the *Hitchman Coal Case* (245 U.S., 229) the United States Supreme Court had validated the "yellow dog" contract, and it was becoming increasingly clear that the protections offered union labor under the Clayton Act did not mean in judicial eyes what labor had thought they meant. In *United Mine Workers* v. *Colorado Coal Company* (259 U.S., 344) a federal court of appeals upheld the decision of a lower court that the union would have to pay triple damages under the Sherman Antitrust Act for calling a strike. In *Duplex Printing Press Co.* v. *Deering* (254 U.S., 443) the Supreme Court held illegal a boycott designed to force the unionization of a factory.

The decision in *American Steel Foundries* v. *Tri-City Central Trades Council* (257 U.S., 184) maintained that the courts might insist on peaceful picketing, even to the extent of requiring one picket only at each entrance to a plant. The first of these cases was decided in 1917, the second in 1919, and the last two in 1921, hence the trend toward the judicial disciplining of labor was well along before the Harding administration and the Taft Supreme Court began to take a hand.[38]

In the election of 1920 the weakness of labor could hardly have been more apparent. Neither the Democrats nor the Republicans minded much what labor had to say, while the attempt to launch a separate labor party failed ludicrously. Debs and the Socialists got a substantial protest vote, but a smaller percentage of the total vote than in 1912. Furthermore, as every intelligent observer could see, the overwhelming triumph of Harding and the reactionaries could not have been accomplished without the help of labor votes. Who, then, really ruled in America? Not the labor unions, for a certainty. Not the federal government under the broken Wilson or the incompetent Harding. Who else, if not the business interests? Later on President Coolidge was to remark sententiously that "The business of America is business." He might also have said that in every important aspect of economic and political life the control of America lay with business.[39]

The
Plight of
Agriculture

The First World War marked a turning point in the history of American agriculture. Before the war "the agrarian myth" had scarcely been challenged. "Agriculture," as Bernard Baruch phrased it, "is the greatest and fundamentally the most important of our American industries. The cities are but the branches of the tree of national life, the roots of which go deeply into the land. We all flourish or decline with the farmer." To be sure, the produce of industry had long exceeded greatly in value the produce of the farm, but it could still be asserted, on the basis of the 1910 census, that country people accounted for well over half the American population; the farmer was still dominant. But times were changing; even without the war a veritable revolution was imminent. For both industry and agriculture the fighting in Europe brought on a war boom, a postwar boom, and then a precipitate decline. The difference was that industry, after a few years in the trough, rose rapidly to new heights, while agriculture was never to be the same again. By the time of the 1920 census the farm population had dropped to about one-third of the total and was still going down, while the gap between industrial wealth and agricultural wealth had widened to a gulf. Tax returns showed that for every dollar that came from the farms American manufacturers returned $72. Not only did farm prosperity virtually disappear for two full decades, but changes in the farmer's way of life diminished his importance as an individual, and turned over to bustling machines, to expanding organizations, and to proliferating governmental agencies prerogatives that had once been his alone.[1]

The war served to delay somewhat the declining status of agriculture and to deceive the farmer into thinking that he had entered upon a new era of prosperity. The fighting had only just begun in 1914 when *Wallace's Farmer,* no doubt speaking the mind of food producers throughout the nation, advised the farmer "to grow all the grain and other food products he can, being assured that there will be a market. England will control the seas; nobody disputes that. Her navy will provide a way for getting our food products safely to Great Britain, Holland, Belgium, and all the countries not yet drawn into the war." The United States should not take sides, but should "make ready to feed the nations." For a consideration, of course. American farmers had the same eager desire for profits that characterized American industrialists. Undoubtedly the war was a catastrophe for civilization, but as long as Europeans saw fit to indulge in such madness, there was no reason why Americans should not turn an honest penny by catering to wartime needs. Long before American entrance into the war, farm incomes had begun to rise, and a period of lush prosperity seemed assured.[2]

The American declaration of war greatly accelerated the process already begun, for now the United States government took a direct hand in stimulating agricultural production. By-passing the Department of Agriculture, which conceivably could have handled the problem, the President chose to set up a new and temporary Food Administration headed by Herbert Hoover, whose activities with the Commission for the Relief of Belgium had already captured the public imagination. Hoover discharged his duties with consummate skill, making excellent use of the patriotic motive to supplement the profit motive. Encouraged by the slogan "Food will win the war," American farmers, despite a diminished labor supply, produced the food required for domestic needs, for the armies at the front, and for the hard-pressed Allies. They brought millions of previously untilled acres under cultivation, especially to grow wheat, the crop in most insistent demand. For the five years that preceded the war the average wheat planting had been 47 million acres; by 1919 it was up to 74 million. Wheat yields during the war period were somewhat irregular, with the billion-bushel crop of 1915 exceeding all others, but the crops of 1918 and 1919 were almost as large. What happened to wheat happened in lesser degree to virtually all food products. The total acreage for growing crops rose about 13 per cent during the war, and the production of meat about 23 per cent. Southern agriculture was less affected by war expansion than the more strictly food-producing areas of the North and West, although the demand for tobacco increased, especially toward the close of the war. Cotton exports fell off precipitately while the fighting lasted, but short crops, a high domestic demand, and inflation sent cotton prices soaring along with the rest.[3]

The government was not content, however, to allow all agricultural prices to seek their own levels. Under the Food and Fuel Control Act of August 10, 1917, the President was given sweeping powers to regulate the production and handling of foodstuffs, including the right to fix prices. As a result, the price of wheat for the 1917 crop was set at $2.20 a bushel, and for the 1918 crop at $2.26. The farmers received these decisions with mingled feelings. On the one hand, they appreciated the existence of a minimum price below which wheat could not fall; on the other, they saw no reason why agricultural prices should not be permitted to rise in accordance with demand, just as retail prices were rising in industry. Why should the raw-producers alone be forced to accept limited profits? Later, when farm prices began to fall, Hoover's part in holding down war profits for the farmers came in for vigorous criticism. Of all the possible presidential candidates in 1920, he was regarded, according to a prominent Grange spokesman, as "the most objectionable to the farmers."[4]

With respect to livestock prices the Food Administration followed a policy that differed somewhat from its wheat policy, but that had essentially similar results. The meat question, Hoover assured the farmers, was quite as critical as the bread question, and the production of fats was a prime necessity. Every pound of fat, he insisted, was "as sure of service as every bullet," and every hog "of greater value to the winning of the war than a shell." Because of the need for fats, and the speed with which pork could be produced in comparison with beef, the Food Administration placed its main emphasis upon hog production, and by way of encouragement promised farmers to keep the price per hundredweight of hogs at thirteen times the price of a bushel of corn, a fair deal in farmers' eyes. But when by the fall of 1918 the market was glutted with hogs, Hoover reneged on his bargain in an indirect fashion that made the farmers furious. The corn-hog ratio, he said, was meant to be computed on the basis of corn prices on the farm, and not, as every farmer had assumed, on the Chicago market. This decision compounded Hoover's unpopularity with the hog producers, who together with other farmers tended to hold more against the Food Administrator than his manipulation of the corn-hog ratio. He had "a mental bias," *Wallace's Farmer* explained, "which causes farmers to distrust him. They look upon him as a typical autocrat of big business —able, shrewd, resourceful, and ready to adopt almost any means to accomplish his end. Farmers do not underestimate Mr. Hoover's ability, but they fear it." Hoover's policy tended at first to stabilize the price of hogs at about $15.50 per hundredweight, and later at about $17.50. It also tended to set the pattern for other livestock prices, which held up well throughout the war. In addition, the Food Administration gave a guarantee on beans and peas, and bought the entire American and Cuban sugar crops at prices (about nine cents a pound) agreed upon with committees of the producers.[5]

With respect to agriculture no less than to industry, altogether too little attention had been given during the war years to the problems that the return of peace would bring. When suddenly, as Walter Weyl phrased it, "the war died on our hands," the United States found itself "about to be deluged with wheat, with hundreds of millions of bushels, with wheat that we cannot sell and cannot eat." Not only was the government obligated under existing pledges to buy up the entire crop of 1918 at the fixed price, but it soon became obvious that for some time to come it would not find it politically feasible to end the price guarantee. In response to farm pressure, Congress by the Wheat Stabilization Act of March 4, 1919, appropriated $1 billion to continue the program until June 1, 1920. The Food Administration was equal to the emergency that this legislation created. Hoover knew that the postwar world would be confronted by "a gigantic food problem," to satisfy which the great stores of American foodstuffs could be used. If the American supplies could only be marketed properly, the guarantees to the farmers could be met, and the country banks that had backed the farmers could be saved. Nor was the problem merely one of wheat; the war program for agriculture had gone too far to be liquidated overnight. If the United States government would only furnish most of the money and credit with which European governments could buy, then the needy European nations could take over our excess produce at whatever prices we might direct. Hoover therefore saw to it that the Food Administration was merged quickly into an Administration for the Relief and Reconstruction of Europe. Obligations contracted by European nations were met for the most part by loans and credits furnished by the United States government, and unavailable in like quantity from any other source. And so for a year and a half after the armistice the flow of American farm products overseas continued unabated. In general, throughout this period the prices of other agricultural products—as well as of wheat—remained at figures far in excess of their prewar levels.[6]

American farmers somehow deluded themselves into thinking that all this new prosperity was to be permanent. It had been dinned into their ears while the war was on that for an indefinite period Europe would be unable to feed herself, that the demand for American foodstuffs would long outlast the war. Exaggerated reports on the depletion of livestock in the warring countries had led farmers to believe that the restoration of meat production overseas would be particularly difficult, and that the demand for American meat would continue for many years to come. Naturally, the current high prices would also survive. They had resulted, some experts said, as much from inflation as from scarcity, and there was no hint that inflation would end. The United States had simply reached a permanently higher price level on which the rewards of farming had happily turned out to be quite comparable to the rewards of industry. "There are no indications so far," commented *Life* ruefully, "that the war prices have any intention of signing an armistice."[7]

The fact that Europe might lack the means with which to buy American produce meant less to most American farmers than now seems reasonable. The need of the war-torn nations for more food and clothing and raw materials than they themselves could supply was obvious; surely the means to supply this need would be found. If necessary, the United States would continue to furnish credits until the European economies were restored. "Can we afford to cut loose from Europe in this time of trial?" asked one farm editor. Another student of the situation suggested the creation of a great American credit organization to accept European securities and sell bonds to investors in the United States; by this means European nations would be able to buy what American producers had to sell. But most American farmers scarcely attempted to think the problem through. Prices were comfortably high and would no doubt stay that way. Mr. Hoover's relief organization would be able to handle the problem temporarily, and the future would take care of itself.[8]

A natural by-product of the high war and postwar prices for farm produce was a devastating land boom. Already in evidence before the signing of the armistice, the boom zoomed along merrily for the next two years. Land values tended to rise the whole country over, although most spectacularly in the corn belt of the Middle West, particularly in the state of Iowa. The value of farm land, new purchasers assumed, depended chiefly upon its earnings, and the expectation was that these earnings would remain high for the predictable future. One rule-of-thumb measurement, based upon many years of corn-belt experience, was that good farm land could be expected to move up from $1 to $2 per acre for each cent of permanent advance in the normal price of corn. Thus, when corn prices rose from a normal prewar level of $0.50 a bushel to $0.70 a bushel, then the price of land might legitimately rise a corresponding $20 to $40 per acre. By 1919, with corn selling at $1.34 and other farm prices correspondingly high, farmers and speculators viewed the future with rosy-tinted glasses. According to one observer, "Iowans believe that land is going higher, and that it can never be bought cheaper than at present. They buy therefore to avoid paying a higher price later on. They say there is but one corn belt to grow corn and hogs and the demand for these products is increasing and will continue to increase."[9]

Real estate operators, who made good profits from every sale, fanned the flames of avarice with all their might. They rode from one Iowa farm to another, persuading some to sell and others to buy. By way of encouragement to the doubtful, they even produced fictitious records of sales and profits. "Half the people here," commented one farmer sadly, "are either land agents or speculators in land. Most of the men have never been farmers, and never will be farmers. The game is to buy and sell, and many are boasting of making thirty or forty thousand dollars in a few months. And then they say the boom is just started. Land has sold around here for $200 an acre until a few months ago and now the price is $300 and better. Some farms have changed hands three or four times with an increase of $10 to $20 per acre each time." About 9 per cent of all the farms in the state, according to another estimate, changed hands at least once during these feverish months.[10]

The boom continued unabated throughout most of the year 1920. By March of that year Iowa land prices, on the average, were up about 166 per cent above 1910 figures and 33 per cent above 1919 figures. This increase on the state's 30 million acres of improved farm land, *Wallace's Farmer* noted, meant that the capital wealth of Iowa had risen within a single year by about $1.5 billion. Local booster clubs, businessmen, bankers, and editors delighted in all this unimpeachable evidence of prosperity. Land values, predicted one optimistic banker, would advance sooner or later to $700 or $800 per acre, crop prices would never revert to their old low figures, and population would increase faster than production. While Iowa was hardest hit by the boom, the other corn-belt states were all seriously affected by it. The South Atlantic states, including the Carolinas and Georgia, also shared generously in the inflation. The least change in land prices occurred in New England and some of the western and southwestern states, but the country over land prices had risen by 1920 on an average about 148 per cent above the 1910 prices and about 10 per cent above those of 1919.[11]

The conviction that flush times had come to stay led to many unfortunate results. Reassured by their record profits, many farmers yielded to the temptation to buy new machinery, erect new buildings, and acquire such luxury items as automobiles and victrolas. An unreasonable number undertook to raise purebred livestock, and bought expensive herds that could not possibly pay out if farm prices should fall. Farmers who had money to invest, whether from savings or from land sales, were easy marks for smooth-talking stock salesmen, who induced them to buy shares in shady oil or mining companies, unsound packing cooperatives, and other get-rich-quick swindles. Often the cash payment on such an investment was not above 25 per cent, with notes for the remainder discounted at the local banks. Well-to-do farmers also bought more land than they could farm, thus adding appreciably to the number of tenant farmers. Indeed, according to a well-demonstrated rule, the prevalence of tenancy rose in direct ratio to land prices. Approximately one-half of the most valuable land in the corn belt thus came to be farmed by renters who paid cash rent at about 70 per cent above prewar rates, and were doomed to failure in case prices went down. Some corn-belt farmers succumbed to the wiles of outside promoters who sold them distant lands at figures that would have been low for Iowa, but were unreasonably high for Texas, or wherever the purchases were located. Thus, all too frequently it was not the farmers who profited from the boom transactions, but someone who took the farmers' money away from them.[12]

Despite the high prices that the farmers received for their produce during and after the war, the land boom was financed largely on credit. Buyers of Iowa farm land paid down on an average less than 6 per cent of the purchase price, and for the rest signed mortgages to be paid over periods varying from five to twenty years. Long-term loans, obtainable at low rates from the Federal Farm Loan Banks of 1916, may have helped set this pattern, but most of the boom-time mortgages were financed by local banks, many of which had been launched only recently by retired farmers and small-business men whose knowledge of banking was quite inadequate. In eleven agricultural states more than 1,700 new banks had begun to operate during the years 1914 to 1920, two or three times as many as the available resources warranted. These financial innocents, in order to build up their profits, actually encouraged farmers to borrow who might better have been paying off their old debts than contracting new and reckless ones.[13]

Much of the blame for the credit situation lay, no doubt, with the easy-money policy that the Federal Reserve Banks had pursued while the land boom was in the making; country bankers found it far too easy to discount their paper. In consequence farm mortgage totals rose to phenomenally high figures, for the country as a whole from $1.6 billion in 1915 to $2.5 billion in 1918 and $3.8 billion in 1920. During this brief period loans and discounts in the principal agricultural states (excluding large city transactions) climbed from $2.5 billion to $5.4 billion. By 1920 the total mortgage debt upon American farms amounted to about one-third of the value of all the nation's farm lands and buildings. The banks, *Wallace's Farmer* observed early in 1920, had overlent, not only to the farmers but to other borrowers also. Should anything unusual happen to make people uneasy, the resulting cancellation of orders and squirming out of contracts would insure a period of ruinous deflation, and the whole ramshackle edifice would collapse.[14]

High prices for farm products and for farm lands, as we have seen, were only part of the general inflation; all prices had risen, and the public outcry against this unpleasant phenomenon grew stronger with each passing month. Complaints against the farmers for the high cost of food led to demands soon after the armistice for an end to the price-fixing program that was still holding wheat and meat at such "fictitious" levels. Only a few months before, complained one corn-belt editor, the daily papers had appealed to the farmer "to work hard and save the world from starvation. Now their chief concern is to beat down the price of farm products, and this without regard to the cost of production." Indeed, city dwellers in general tended to place a quite unreasonable proportion of the blame for the ever higher cost of living upon farmer avarice.[15]

Farmer spokesmen tried in vain to educate the public in the facts of farm life. The cost of farm labor was up along with other labor costs. The higher prices of farm land had added ten or fifteen cents a bushel to the cost of producing corn, and equivalent amounts for other farm products. Interest rates had risen, and a great many farmers had to make payments on much higher mortgages than they had owed before the war. Higher land values had also meant higher taxes, a charge that the farmer could not escape, for his assets were all in plain sight of the assessor. Furthermore, the high cost of living was not restricted to the city dweller; it hit the farmer, too, raising the prices of everything he had to buy—machinery, fuel, harness, fencing, fertilizer, and all the rest. A price level less than 70 per cent above the prewar normal, one observer maintained, would ruin nearly every recent purchaser of land, and would drive many other farmers out of business. Owner-operators were perhaps a little better off than tenants, for cash rentals were extremely high, and without high prices for their crops tenant farmers had nowhere else to go but broke.[16]

The prospective ending of governmental price guarantees in midsummer, 1920, was less frightening to the farmers than it should have been. Most of them had long associated price fixing with the idea of keeping prices down; the purpose of the government program, they had come to believe, was to prevent the farmer from getting as high prices, relatively, as other economic interests had received. It was a long time before the average farmer could see any good in price fixing, and for years he tended to denounce it with more fervor than logic. What the farmers did see, whether it existed or not, was a conspiracy of government and bankers to force prices down and to make agricultural producers bear the chief brunt of the burden. The government was tightening up credit by buying back its own bonds at discount rates, by June, 1920, $1,043 million worth of them for $933 million. Why, instead of this somewhat unethical transaction, could there not at least have been some relief from taxation? The steady raising of rediscount rates by the Federal Reserve Banks, which occurred throughout the fall and winter of 1919-1920, seemed also deliberately designed to bring grief to the farmers. This was the time of year when they needed credit to hold their crops off the market; without it, they would have to sell at harvest time, or thereabouts, at prices forced down by the glutted markets. Loose-lipped bankers frankly proclaimed that "they did not propose to loan any money to farmers to enable them to hold their crops." One banker went so far as to say that "after election his bank proposed to call in farm paper and to see to it that wheat and other commodities came down to where they belong. He added that the farmer needed to be shown his place once more almost as badly as did labor."[17]

It proved almost futile for the farmers to protest, as they did, that they were not wholly, or even chiefly, responsible for the high prices that retailers charged. According to Senator Capper of Kansas, profits taken after the farmer sold his produce and before it reached the ultimate consumer accounted for 70 per cent of the final sale price. The cost of a mutton chop in a New York hotel was greater than the sale price of an entire sheep in Kansas, while a bushel of Michigan potatoes worth one dollar on the farm paid six profits before it sold in Washington, D. C., for four or five dollars. Why blame the farmers for the nation's wasteful system of distribution? Why not instead concentrate on the speculators who hoarded foodstuffs in warehouses and cold-storage plants precisely for the purpose of sending prices up? For this kind of holding, the bankers had plenty of credit, but not for the farmers who wished to avoid selling on a glutted market.[18]

The lengths to which the authorities, both state and national, were willing to go in order to bring farm prices down filled the farmers with anger and dismay. State officials tried to invoke the antitrust laws against milk producers in the Chicago district who combined forces in order to retain for themselves a slightly larger fraction of the price paid by consumers for a quart of milk. The Interstate Commerce Commission permitted railroad rates, already too high to suit the farmers, to go up again as soon as the roads were returned to private ownership, thus insuring another addition to the high cost of foodstuffs, or another cut in prices paid to the farmers, whichever won out. According to Herbert Quick, the new farm schedules that the railroads announced were utterly intolerable. "If a committee of madmen had been summoned from the nearest insane asylum to make a freight schedule, they could not have done worse." Unkindest cut of all was the sale by the government at reduced rates of army surpluses, including canned meats, with the deliberate intention of competing with current production. The farmer had created these surpluses as a matter of patriotism; now the excess so produced was to be "used as a club to beat down low farm prices still lower."[19]

Beginning in the summer of 1920 farm prices went down all right, even if the farmers had the reasons for the decline somewhat out of focus. The removal of price guarantees as of May 31, 1920, the end of deficit financing, the unwillingness of the American government to continue foreign loans, the revival of European agriculture, and the increasing ability of other non-European nations to compete in the world's markets accounted principally for the ever lower prices at which American farmers were obliged to sell. The whole American price structure was in for a disastrous collapse, but the farmers were the first to feel the pressure. In July, 1920, the index of farm prices went down ten points below the June index; in August it dropped fifteen points more, and in September still another fifteen points. During the month of October when crop sales were normally at their peak, prices for the principal crops declined 19.1 per cent, as against an average of only 3.8 per cent during the same month in the preceding ten years. November showed an even greater decline. Crop yields in 1920 were high, and the fact that so many bankers were unable, or refused, to furnish farmers the credit they needed to hold their produce off the market certainly had something to do with forcing prices downward. By the end of the year the level of the principal farm prices was only a small fraction above prewar figures, and within another year even that fraction had been wiped out. By this time wheat and beef cattle were actually selling for less than in 1914, the former down from $0.986 a bushel to $0.927, the latter from $6.01 a hundredweight to $4.62. According to one estimate, in the year ending January 21, 1921, American farmers lost on beef cattle not only all they had gained during the war, but 50 per cent more. About the only consolation in the situation was the fact that at the low prices farm products did generally move, the dollar proceeds were smaller, but the physical volume of sales kept up.[20]

The fact that the price decline on farm produce both preceded and exceeded the decline in other prices hurt the farmer both in his pocketbook and in his state of mind. When farm prices were approaching their prewar levels, pig iron was still up by 264 per cent and petroleum by 313 per cent. Retail prices stayed up long after wholesale prices had begun to slump, and for many months the prices of what the farmer had to buy contrasted ever more sharply with the prices of what he had to sell. With farm income thus drastically curtailed, how was the farmer to pay his debts and keep on purchasing necessary equipment and supplies? At their worst, non-agricultural prices rarely dropped to below one and one-half times the level of prewar prices, and so the disparity between them and farm prices continued on indefinitely. In 1919, for example, a bushel of corn would buy five gallons of gasoline; in 1921 maybe not even a gallon. In 1919 six bushels of corn would buy a ton of coal; in 1921 it would take perhaps sixty bushels. No wonder Nebraska farmers were beginning to burn corn for fuel as they had done in the days of Populism. In 1921 a given volume of farm products bought only about three-fourths as much manufactured goods as in 1914. The cotton farmers of the South were no better off than the food producers of the North and West. By the end of 1920 cotton was bringing only about 15 cents a pound, and by June, 1921, it was down to 10.3 cents, well below prewar levels and below the cost of production. Southern farm leaders helplessly pled for a 50 per cent reduction in cotton acreage and a 50 per cent increase in food and feed crops.[21]

The collapse in farm prices soon brought the land boom to an unseemly end. Bankruptcies multiplied, particularly in the areas of marginal land that the high wartime profits had induced rash investors to open up. There were bankruptcies in business, also, but farm bankruptcies by 1920 were outrunning other bankruptcies in about the proportion of 9 to 5; in the succeeding months the proportion got worse rather than better. Forced sales of Iowa real estate in 1921 showed a drop in land prices of 50 per cent. Farmers who had sold out and collected at high prices were in luck, but often they were no longer farmers. Those who had bought at high prices and those who had sold on credit were less fortunate. One subscriber to *Wallace's Farmer* set forth in a letter to the editor a typical situation. He had bought a quarter section of land at $300 per acre, paying down $9,000, or less than 20 per cent, and signing a fifteen-year mortgage at 5 per cent for the remainder. He had also made some expensive improvements on his place. Came January, 1921, and he found himself owing $2,000 for interest and taxes but, because of the low prices he had received for his crops, without the money he needed to meet his obligations. What was he to do? Thousands of other farmers were in the same predicament or worse. Some of them gave up and quit farming. Some stayed on as tenants, often on the very farms they had once thought they owned. Those who could negotiate further loans did so, and gambled on the future, but many of them lost. During the postwar deflation farm bankruptcies reached a total of 453,000.[22]

For the farmers who tried to hold on, borrowing had become extremely difficult. The Federal Reserve Board had laid down the law. "The expansion of credit set in motion by the war," it had intoned, "must be checked." And checked it was. This policy meant that not only the farmers who had borrowed to buy were in trouble, but also the bankers who held farm mortgages. An epidemic of bank failures began that was to last throughout the 1920's. Up in North Dakota, where the farm economy was geared to wheat, there were 17 bank failures during the year 1920. On the one hand, farmer patrons could not sell their products for enough to pay their debts; on the other, the Federal Reserve Board had cut off the country bankers' supply of credit. Soon the number of bank failures for the country as a whole began to mount. The number in 1922 was 367; in 1926 it was 976; by 1930 it was 1,345, and still going up. Unsurprisingly, small country banks which had served the farmers accounted for a disproportionate share of these failures.[23]

The depression for agriculture was no short-lived affair. Unlike industry, which was down for only about two years, agriculture continued in the doldrums throughout the decade, and longer. The farmers worked on doggedly and harvests were good, but farm prices remained far below the cost of production. The root of the farmers' difficulty was their inability to control production. Manufacturers could tailor their output to meet estimated demands, but the farmers had no such advantage. They were individualists, and by tradition they grew all that they could grow. No means had yet been found to force them to cut down on production; indeed, the lower prices fell, the larger the crops they thought they must raise to meet their existing fixed charges. They had expanded their acreages because of a special wartime need. Now that the need was gone, they found themselves producing an annual excess far beyond the requirements of American consumers. The only way to dispose of this excess was to sell it abroad at whatever prices it would bring. But the prices that American farmers were able to get for this "exportable surplus," sold on the world market in competition with foreign producers, set the prices for all the rest. And the prices thus set were not high enough to enable American farmers to pay their debts and live decently. This was the heart of the farm problem.[24]

Both business and labor found it easier to organize for self-defense than did agriculture. Indeed, only in times of great stress and strain were American farmers able to forget their much vaunted individualism enough to work together with any degree of effectiveness. Even then they generally suffered much from what might be called commodity consciousness. Wheat farmers, for example, tended to have a strong prejudice against corn farmers, while those who raised grain or livestock recognized few common interests with the growers of cotton or tobacco. Geography magnified still further the problem of farmer cooperation, with sectional differences forever raising formidable obstacles in the way of agreements.[25]

But the course of events that led to the collapse of farm prices in the fall and winter of 1920-1921 did much to promote the cause of farmer solidarity. Older and somewhat moribund orders such as the Grange, the

Farmers' Union, and the American Society of Equity came actively to life, while the Non-Partisan League of North Dakota threatened for a time to spread over all the Northwest. The most pressing need of the farmers, many of their apologists believed, was for some kind of overall federation that would do for agriculture what the United States Chamber of Commerce was doing for business, and what the American Federation of Labor was doing for labor. Why not a National Chamber of Agriculture? "Labor is adequately represented and has great influence in Washington," *Wallace's Farmer* complained. "Various organizations of capitalists, manufacturers and business organizations of all kinds are well represented there," but, by way of contrast, the collective voice of the farmers could hardly be heard. This idea was by no means new, and there were several rival efforts to meet the need. But the organization that won out was the American Farm Bureau Federation, formed in 1919 on the well-laid foundations of the county-agent system, and the growing number of State Farm Bureaus.[26]

The uneven struggle of the farmers to achieve equality with business and labor lasted on into the period of Republican ascendancy and need not concern us here. It was far easier to diagnose the farmers' ills than to prescribe remedies for them, but some of the suggestions that were to win favor later on were already under consideration. By way of self-help, the idea of crop withholding, which was strongly urged both by the Farmers' Union and by Equity, gained considerable favor. On the assumption that middlemen and speculators made huge profits by buying at harvest time when prices were low, and selling later on when prices had risen, the farmers of Kansas staged something akin to a wheat strike late in 1920, but the inadequacy of farm credit seriously

handicapped this and all similar undertakings. Cooperative marketing was a kind of projection of the holding
movement; what farmers could not do individually they
might accomplish by agencies of their own creation. This,
also, was a well-worn thought, but the belief that it might
solve the marketing problem grew steadily stronger, and
was destined to be given a serious tryout during the coming decade. There was talk, too, of crop restrictions and
acreage limitations, but the means of enforcing any such
agreements upon literally millions of individuals lay well
outside the experience of the times.[27]

Pressure politics was a natural result when other
means failed. Farm pressure in favor of the continued
extension of government credit to foreign purchasers of
American goods led to the re-establishment early in 1921
of the War Finance Corporation, but Congress had to
pass the measure over the outgoing President's veto, and
steps to implement the decision taken awaited the incom-
ing Harding administration. The farmers demanded, also,
protective tariffs to keep out Canadian wheat, Argentine
corn, and other foreign products; to this end they persuaded Congress to pass an emergency agricultural tariff
bill. But this measure, too, met a Presidential veto, and
this time the veto was sustained. In Wilson's opinion,
agricultural tariffs would do little to provide the relief
sought. What the farmer really needed was "a better
system of domestic marketing and credit," together with
"larger foreign markets for his surplus products," ends
that could not be served by the erection of "high trade
barriers." The farmers were slow to understand why the
kind of protective tariffs that helped manufacturers would
not also help them, but they agreed with Wilson on the
subject of agricultural credits, and demanded that as a
start in the right direction there should be one or two

farmer members of the Federal Reserve Board. Livestock farmers were much agitated over the monopolistic tendencies of the great packing companies, and insisted upon legislation to guarantee a fair, open, and competitive market. And so on. But in actual fact neither the farmers nor the government had as yet discovered a plausible overall agricultural policy. McNary-Haugenism, the export debenture plan, the Triple A, and parity prices were all some distance in the future.[28]

There was some agitation in 1920 for the founding of a third party. The program of the National Non-Partisan League, despite its disclaimers, pointed in this direction, and some farmers favored it. Also, a faction of labor hoped to create a united farmer-labor front, while a Committee of Forty-eight, representing what was left of the old 1912 Progressive organization, was eager to cooperate in any endeavor that might lead to independent political action. But at a complicated Chicago convention the labor faction, influenced possibly by a few unconfessed Communists, refused to make the compromises necessary to induce Robert M. LaFollette of Wisconsin to accept a third party nomination. Out of the tumult there emerged eventually a Farmer-Labor ticket, minus farmer support, and with an unknown candidate for President, Parley P. Christensen of Utah, who won only a handful of votes in the election.[29]

Logical as it might seem for the farmers and the workers, having common antagonists, to unite, the fact was that the forces of agriculture and of labor were in many ways competitive. The farmers wanted high prices for their produce, while the workers wanted low prices for food. The workers wanted high wages, while the farmers wanted low-cost manufactured goods. The farmers were small capitalists, or at least aspired to be, while the workers were by definition employees. It was not a simple matter to bring two such divergent groups together. In the election of 1920 the farmers, except in the South, tended to join the majority of the voters in casting their ballots for Harding. They held many grievances against the Wilson administration, and their aspirations were on the whole better recognized in the Republican than in the Democratic platform. They thus did their part toward turning over the federal government to the business interests whose wishes were to be paramount in the new administration.[30]

And now, to sum up. Avoiding complexities, there were three principal pressure groups in American society during the postwar years, business, labor, and agriculture. Of these three, business was completely in the ascendancy. It had emerged from the war stronger than it had ever been before, and even the advent of a postwar depression did not diminish its leadership. Agriculture, once so dominant in American life, was definitely on the decline. The business interests, according to an eminent economist, had "set themselves up as an arrogant oligarchy," and had demanded that "agriculture should be a humble serving class," to be exploited for the food and raw products it could produce, just as imperialistic powers had once exploited their colonial possessions.[31] Labor, likewise, was at low ebb. The spectacular gains it had made during the war disappeared with the unsuccessful strikes of 1919 and the "Red scare" of 1920. For the workers no less than for the farmers, the ruling industrialists had prescribed only an inferior and supplementary role—theirs not to reason why.

Under different circumstances the government might have undertaken to hold the balance among these competing forces, and to defend the rights of the public at large. But after the war the powers of government had declined precipitately, and the will to exercise regulatory authority over business had all but disappeared. Wilson's illness, the economic principles of such governmental agents as Houston, Palmer, and Hoover, and the Republican victories in the elections of 1918 had conspired to turn the government over to the very business interests it was supposed to restrain, with business the senior partner and government the junior partner in a common undertaking. After the advent of the Harding administration this transformation was even more marked. For a dozen years there was no serious divergence between what the government did and what the business interests wanted done.

It is not unreasonable to assume that the postwar boom and collapse of 1919-1920 resulted not only from the war, but also from the ineptitude of business and of business-dominated governmental leadership. As for the quick recovery and the business boom that marked the middle 1920's, business claimed full responsibility for that, and the claim need not be disputed. But just as the little postwar boom had led to a little collapse, so the big boom of the 1920's led to a big collapse. Did not the blame lie chiefly with the determination of business to have its own way, and the unwillingness or inability of government to resist business pressure? Had the nation's leaders had the wit to see and understand what had happened in the two postwar years, might they not have averted the disaster that overtook the country in 1929? In other words, were not the lessons that history was so eager to teach overlooked as usual?

Notes
to the
Chapters

Business and Government

1. Frederic L. Paxson, *Postwar Years: Normalcy, 1918-1923* (Berkeley, Calif., 1948), pp. 4-5, 116-117, 121-122.

2. John Morton Blum, *The Republican Roosevelt* (Cambridge, Mass., 1954), pp. 1-6, and *passim;* Arthur S. Link, *Woodrow Wilson and the Progressive Era, 1910-1917* (New York, 1954), pp. 34-35, and *passim.*

3. Lincoln Colcord, "The Breakdown of Government," *The Nation,* CIX (Dec. 13, 1919), 743; *Journal of Commerce and Commercial Bulletin,* May 19, 1920, p. 6, col. 1-2; *Life,* LXXIII (Feb. 6, 1919), 200, 202, 213, 216.

4. David F. Houston, *Eight Years with Wilson's Cabinet* (Garden City, N.Y., 1926), II, 37-39, 64-69; *The New Republic,* XXI (Jan. 14, 1920), 180; Harold Laski, *The American Democracy* (New York, 1948), p. 117.

5. *The Nation,* CIX (Nov. 29, 1919), 675.

6. Harold E. Stearns (ed.), *Civilization in the United States* (New York, 1922), p. 24.

7. Historical Branch, War Plans Division, General Staff, *A Handbook of Economic Agencies of the War of 1917* (Washington, 1919), pp. 211, 496; Waldo G. Leland and Newton D. Mereness (eds.), *Introduction to the American Official Sources for the Eco-*

nomic and Social History of the World War (New Haven, 1926), pp. 377, 399, 411; Walker D. Hines, War History of American Railroads (New Haven, 1928), p. 220; United States Statutes at Large (Washington, 1921), XLI, 988-1008.

8. Walter Weyl, "Planless Demobilization," New Republic, XVII (Nov. 30, 1918), 125-127; New Republic, XVIII (Feb. 22, 1919), 105; Paxson, Postwar Years, pp. 6-7; War Department, Annual Reports, 1919 (Washington, 1920), I, 13-20; James R. Mock and Evangeline Thurber, Report on Demobilization (Norman, Okla., 1944), pp. 132-136.

9. Bernard M. Baruch, American Industry in the War (New York, 1941), pp. 105-107; John Dewey, "The New Paternalism," New Republic, XVII (Dec. 21, 1918), 216-217.

10. Howard Burton, "The Business Man and the Future," New Republic, XVII (Dec. 21, 1918), pp. 220-221.

11. Baruch, American Industry in the War, pp. 105-107; Margaret L. Coit, Mr. Baruch (Boston, 1957), pp. 220-221.

12. Colcord, in The Nation, p. 744; Paxson, Postwar Years, pp. 87-88; Ray Stannard Baker and William E. Dodd (eds.), The Public Papers of Woodrow Wilson (New York, 1927), V, 313.

13. Public Papers of Woodrow Wilson, V, 315; Weyl, "Buffer Employment," New Republic, XVII (Dec. 7, 1918), 159-163; Hard, "The Meaning of Reconstruction," ibid., (Dec. 14, 1918), 183.

14. New Republic, XVII (Nov. 30, 1918), 125-127; XVIII (Feb. 22, 1919), 105; Paul A. Samuelson and Everett E. Hagen, After the War— 1918-1920, National Resources Planning Board pamphlet (Washington, 1943), pp. 5-6.

15. Frederic L. Paxson, America at War, 1917-1918 (Boston, 1939), pp. 76-77; Coit, Mr. Baruch, pp. 215-216; George Soule, Prosperity Decade: From War to Depression, 1917-1929 (New York, 1947), p. 81.

16. Soule, Prosperity Decade, p. 83; Mock and Thurber, Report on Demobilization, pp. 145-163; Samuelson and Hagen, After the War, pp. 6-10, 38.

17. Samuelson and Hagen, After the War, pp. 7, 12-13, 38; William Hard in New Republic, XVII (Dec. 14, 1918), 182-183.

18. Soule, Prosperity Decade, pp. 83-84; Simon Kuznets, National Product in Wartime, National Bureau of Economic Research (New York, 1945), p. 134; Samuelson and Hagen, After the War, pp. 11-15.

19. Samuelson and Hagen, After the War, pp. 16-17; Simon Kuznets, National Income and Its Composition, 1919-36, National Bureau of Economic Research (New York, 1941), I, 137; Soule, Prosperity Decade, pp. 85-86.

20. Soule, *Prosperity Decade,* pp. 86-88; Harold G. Moulton and Leo Pasvolsky, *War Debts and World Prosperity* (Washington, 1932), pp. 38-42; Samuelson and Hagen, *After the War,* pp. 21-25, 26.

21. Samuelson and Hagen, *After the War,* pp. 6-7, 30; W. G. McAdoo, *Crowded Years* (Boston, 1931), p. 495; Paxson, *America at War,* pp. 366-367; *The Nation,* CVIII (May 17, 1919), 775-776.

22. *The Nation,* CVIII (May 31, 1919), p. 884; Moulton and Pasvolsky, *War Debts,* p. 428; Samuelson and Hagen, *After the War,* pp. 21-22.

23. Samuelson and Hagen, *After the War,* pp. 24-25, 32; Soule, *Prosperity Decade,* pp. 52, 88-89.

24. Soule, *Prosperity Decade,* pp. 86-87; Moulton and Pasvolsky, *War Debts,* p. 39; Herbert Hoover, *The Memoirs of Herbert Hoover,* Vol. I, *Years of Adventure, 1874-1920* (New York, 1951), pp. 300-303; *The Nation,* CIX (Dec. 13, 1919), 732; *The New York Times,* Dec. 6, 1920, p. 12, col. 1; Samuelson and Hagen, *After the War,* pp. 27-28.

25. Samuelson and Hagen, *After the War,* pp. 29-33, 39; George Soule and Vincent P. Carosso, *American Economic History* (New York, 1957), p. 514; Soule, *Prosperity Decade,* pp. 90-91.

26. Soule, *Prosperity Decade,* pp. 91-93, 101; Samuelson and Hagen, *After the War,* pp. 4, 10, 13-15, 31-34; *The Nation,* CIX (Aug. 9, 1919), 158; (Aug. 16, 1919), 197; *Journal of Commerce and Commercial Bulletin,* May 10, 1920, p. 6, col. 1; *The New York Times,* Nov. 1, 1920, p. 1, col. 7; Mark Sullivan, *Our Times: The United States, 1900-1925,* Vol. VI, *The Twenties* (New York, 1935), pp. 165-166.

27. Sullivan, *The Twenties,* p. 167; Frederic C. Miller, *Prices in Recession and Recovery* (New York, 1936), pp. 10, 40-41; Soule and Carosso, *American Economic History,* p. 515; Soule, *Prosperity Decade,* p. 96; Samuelson and Hagen, *After the War,* pp. 15, 34, 39; *Life,* LXXIII (Apr. 3, 1919), 586.

28. Samuelson and Hagen, *After the War,* pp. 15, 23, 34-35; Soule, *Prosperity Decade,* p. 97.

29. Soule, *Prosperity Decade,* pp. 97-99; Samuelson and Hagen, *After the War,* pp. 34-39; W. H. Steiner, *Money and Banking* (New York, 1933), pp. 697, 873-880; *The Outlook,* CXXVIII (July 13, 1921), 454-457.

30. Charles M. Schwab, "What Does Business Want from the Government?" *Collier's,* LXVI (Dec. 11, 1920), 36; Houston, *Eight Years,* II, 100-101; *New Republic,* XIX (May 31, 1919), 132; XXII (Mar. 17, 1920), 74; (May 5, 1920), 304; *The New York Times,* Mar. 5, 1920, p. 1, col. 6; Mar. 11, 1920, p. 1, col. 1; June 30, 1920, p. 20, col. 4.

31. *The New York Times,* Dec. 6, 1920, p. 12, col. 1; *New Republic,* XXV (Dec. 22, 1920), 97; *Nation's Business,* IX (Jan., 1921), 40; Herbert Hoover, "To Break the Vicious Circle," *Nation's Business,* IX (Feb., 1921), 17.

32. Hoover, in *Nation's Business,* p. 25; Schwab, in *Collier's,* p. 34; Sullivan, *The Twenties,* pp. 538-539; *New Republic,* XXII (Mar. 10, 1920), 41-42; (Mar. 17, 1920), 73.

33. *New Republic,* XXII (May 5, 1920), 304; Schwab, in *Collier's,* pp. 7-8, 34, 36; *Nation's Business,* IX (Mar.

1921), 67; Frank E. Hill, "Enter Aerial Commerce," *New Republic,* XVIII (Feb. 1, 1919), 21-23; G. W. Dyer, "Government and Business," in National Association of Manufacturers, *Proceedings, 1922* (New York, 1922), pp. 134-135.

34. James Warren Prothro, *The Dollar Decade; Business Ideas in the 1920's* (Baton Rouge, La., 1954), pp. 88-89.

35. Karl Schriftgiesser, *This Was Normalcy* (Boston, 1948), pp. 12-17, 84-85; Frederick Lewis Allen, *Only Yesterday* (New York, 1931), pp. 159-171, 316-319, 337-338.

The Role of Labor

1. Samuel Gompers, *American Labor and the War* (New York, 1919), pp. 294-295; Frederic L. Paxson, *America at War, 1917-1918* (Boston, 1939), pp. 25-26.

2. Samuel Gompers, *Seventy Years of Life and Labor* (New York, 1957), p. 316; *The New Republic,* XVII (Dec. 7, 1918), 155-156.

3. Paul H. Douglas, *Real Wages in the United States, 1890-1926* (Boston, 1930), p. 391; George Soule, *Prosperity Decade: From War to Depression, 1917-1929* (New York, 1947), pp. 187-188.

4. Soule, *Prosperity Decade,* pp. 57-58, 64-65, 81, 83; Simon Kuznets, *National Product in Wartime* (New York, 1945), p. 145; James R. Mock and

Evangeline Thurber, *Report on Demobilization* (Norman, Okla., 1944), pp. 132-135.

5. Mock and Thurber, *Report on Demobilization,* pp. 181-182; Soule, *Prosperity Decade,* pp. 82-83; E. J. Howenstein, Jr., "Lessons of World War I," *Annals of the American Academy of Political and Social Science,* CCXXXVIII (Mar., 1945), 183-185; U.S. Department of Labor, *Proceedings of the Conference of Governors . . . and Mayors* (Washington, 1919), p. 86; *The New York Times,* Mar. 4, 1919, p. 1, col. 1; Mar. 5, 1919, p. 7, col. 3.

6. Soule, *Prosperity Decade,* pp. 83-84, 221; Douglas, *Real Wages,* p. 391; *Life,* LXXIII (Jan. 9, 1919), 67.

7. *The New Republic*, XVII (Nov. 30, 1918), 123; (Dec. 7, 1918), 155-156; (Dec. 21, 1918), 221; *The American Review of Reviews*, XLIX (Mar., 1919), 334-336; *The Nation*, CIX (July 19, 1919), 72; Lewis L. Lorwin, *The American Federation of Labor* (Washington, 1933), pp. 173-179.

8. *Life*, LXXIII (May 8, 1919), 810; Soule, *Prosperity Decade*, pp. 187-188; *New Republic*, XVII (Nov. 30, 1918), 123; Gompers, *Seventy Years*, pp. 316-317.

9. Charles Patrick Sweeney, "Gompers Triumphant," *The Nation*, CVIII (June 8, 1919), 1002-1003; *The Nation*, CVIII (May 24, 1919), 821; *New Republic*, XVII (Jan. 25, 1919), 364-367; XVIII (Mar. 22, 1919), 247-249; (Apr. 26, 1919), 397-400; XXII (May 5, 1920), 313.

10. *Literary Digest*, LXII (Aug. 16, 1919), 9-10; (Sept. 13, 1919), 140-142; *The Independent*, XCIX (Aug. 16, 1919), 212; *The Nation*, CIX (Aug. 16, 1919), 196; Soule, *Prosperity Decade*, pp. 197-198.

11. Mock and Thurber, *Report on Demobilization*, pp. 56-57, 84-88, 101; Mark Sullivan, *Our Times: The United States, 1900-1925*, Vol. VI, *The Twenties* (New York, 1935), pp. 156-158; David J. Saposs, "Labor," *American Journal of Sociology*, XXXIV (July, 1928), 78-79; Matthew Josephson, *Sidney Hillman:*

Statesman of American Labor (New York, 1952), pp. 184-193.

12. Selig Perlman and Philip Taft, *Labor Movements*, Vol. IV, *History of Labor in the United States, 1896-1932*, ed. John R. Commons (New York, 1935), pp. 439-442; Frederic L. Paxson, *Postwar Years: Normalcy, 1918-1923* (Berkeley, Calif., 1948), 31; William Macdonald, "The Seattle Strike and Afterwards," *The Nation*, CVIII (Mar. 29, 1919), 469-470.

13. Perlman and Taft, *Labor Movements*, pp. 447-449; Sullivan, *The Twenties*, p. 161.

14. William Allen White, *A Puritan in Babylon; The Story of Calvin Coolidge* (New York, 1938), pp. 154-167; Paxson, *Postwar Years*, pp. 98-100; Arthur Warner, "The End of Boston's Police Strike," *The Nation*, CIX (Dec. 20, 1919), 790-792; *The Nation*, CIX (Nov. 8, 1919), 575.

15. Soule, *Prosperity Decade*, pp. 191-192; Interchurch World Movement, *Report on the Steel Strike of 1919* (New York, 1920), pp. 11-19; John A. Fitch, "A Strike for Freedom," *Survey*, XLII (Sept. 27, 1919), 891-892. The entire issue of *Survey*, XLIII (Nov. 8, 1919), is devoted to the steel strike.

16. Perlman and Taft, *Labor Movements*, pp. 461-462; William Z. Foster, *The Great Steel Strike and Its Lessons* (New York, 1920), pp. 16-25, and *Pages from a Worker's*

Life (New York, 1939), pp. 15-161; *Who's Who in America,* XXV (1948-1949), 835.

17. Perlman and Taft, *Labor Movements,* pp. 462-464; Foster, *The Great Steel Strike,* pp. 25, 77-95.

18. Foster, *The Great Steel Strike,* pp. 96-109; *The Nation,* CIX (Dec. 20, 1919), 784.

19. Perlman and Taft, *Labor Movements,* pp. 465-468; Ida M. Tarbell, *The Life of Elbert H. Gary: The Story of Steel* (New York, 1925), pp. 279-316; William Hard, "After the Strike," *New Republic,* XXI (Jan. 28, 1920), pp. 260-261.

20. McAlister Coleman, *Men and Coal* (New York, 1943), p. 90; Anna Rochester, *Labor and Coal* (New York, 1931), pp. 20-25; Stanley J. Jacobs, "Opposition to John L. Lewis within the United Mine Workers of America, 1919-1923" (unpublished Master's thesis, University of California, Berkeley, 1948), p. 4; Perlman and Taft, *Labor Movements,* p. 469.

21. Historical Branch, War Plans Division, General Staff, *A Handbook of Economic Agencies of the War of 1917* (Washington, 1919), p. 179; Perlman and Taft, *Labor Movements,* p. 471; Saul Alinsky, *John L. Lewis: An Unauthorized Biography* (New York, 1949), pp. 29-31.

22. Alinsky, *John L. Lewis,* 32-35; *The Nation,* CIX (Nov. 8, 1919), 577; (Dec. 13, 1919), 734; (Dec. 20, 1919),

787; Jacobs, "Opposition to John L. Lewis," pp. 52-55.

23. Perlman and Taft, *Labor Movements,* p. 472.

24. Perlman and Taft, *Labor Movements,* p. 428; Sullivan, *The Twenties,* p. 513; *The Nation,* CIX (Nov. 15, 1919), 629; *New Republic,* XXII (Apr. 14, 1920), 220.

25. Paul Frederick Brissenden, *The I.W.W.: A Study of American Syndicalism* (New York, 1919), pp. 67, 102, 349; Perlman and Taft, *Labor Movements,* p. 420.

26. Perlman and Taft, *Labor Movements,* pp. 429-430; John S. Gambs, *The Decline of the I.W.W.* (New York, 1932), pp. 26-53.

27. Nathan Fine, *Labor and Farmer Parties in the United States, 1828-1928* (New York, 1928), pp. 347-357; David A. Shannon, *The Socialist Party of America* (New York, 1955), pp. 126-149; Irving Howe and Lewis Coser, *The American Communist Party: A Critical History* (Boston, 1957), pp. 68-69, 90, 105-106.

28. Sullivan, *The Twenties,* pp. 170-171, 176-178; Frederick Lewis Allen, *Only Yesterday* (New York, 1931), pp. 49-52, 71-75.

29. Allen, *Only Yesterday,* pp. 57-58; United States Senate, 65th Cong., 3d Sess., *Bolshevik Propaganda: Hearings before a Sub-committee of the Committee on the Judiciary* (Washington, 1919), I, *passim; United States Statutes at Large* (Washington, 1917,

1919), XXXIX, 874, XLX, 1012; Paxson, *Postwar Years*, pp. 90-91; Fine, *Labor and Farmer Parties*, pp. 352-353; Mercer Green Johnston, "An Open Letter to Attorney-General Palmer," *New Republic*, XXI (Jan. 28, 1920), 264-266; *New Republic*, XXII (May 12, 1920), 325.

30. Sullivan, *The Twenties*, pp. 172-176; Felix Frankfurter, *The Case of Sacco and Vanzetti* (Boston, 1927), pp. 3-8; G. Louis Joughin and Edmund M. Morgan, *The Legacy of Sacco and Vanzetti* (New York, 1948), pp. 3-25.

31. Fine, *Labor and Farmer Parties*, pp. 357-362; James Oneal and G. A. Werner, *American Communism* (New York, 1947), p. 229.

32. Oneal and Werner, *American Communism*, pp. 67n., 285; Howe and Coser, *American Communist Party*, pp. 91-92.

33. Sullivan, *The Twenties*, p. 172; Paxson, *Postwar Years*, pp. 30-31; Allen, *Only Yester-*

day, p. 58; Shannon, *Socialist Party*, pp. 150-154.

34. Soule, *Prosperity Decade*, pp. 83-84, 200.

35. Letter from James R. Day to E. H. Gary, Feb. 2, 1921, Day Papers, Syracuse University; Philip Taft, *The A. F. of L. in the Time of Gompers* (New York, 1957), pp. 401-403.

36. Soule, *Prosperity Decade*, pp. 200-202.

37. Howard Burton, "The Business Man and His Future," *New Republic*, XVII (Dec. 21, 1918), 221; *New Republic*, XIX (June 25, 1919), 241-243.

38. Soule, *Prosperity Decade*, pp. 205-207; Felix Frankfurter, "The President's Industrial Conference," *New Republic*, XXII (Apr. 7, 1920). 179-182.

39. Herbert Harris, *American Labor* (New Haven, 1939), pp. 374-376; Taft, *The A. F. of L.*, pp. 403-404; Shannon, *Socialist Party*, pp. 155-158.

The Plight of Agriculture

1. Richard Hofstadter, *The Age of Reform* (New York, 1955), pp. 31-32; James H. Shideler, *Farm Crisis, 1919-1923* (Berkeley, Calif., 1957), pp. 1-4; *LaFollette's Magazine*, XII (Aug., 1920), 117.

2. *Wallace's Farmer*, XXXIX (Sept. 11, 1914), 1221; (Sept. 25, 1914), 1284; A. B. Genung, "Agriculture in the World War Period," United

States Department of Agriculture, *Yearbook, 1940* (Washington, 1940), pp. 278-279.

3. Genung, in U.S.D.A., *Yearbook, 1940*, pp. 283-285, 289.

4. *Ibid.*, pp. 282-283; Shideler, *Farm Crisis*, pp. 23-24; Theodore Saloutos and John D. Hicks, *Agricultural Discontent in the Middle West, 1900-*

1939 (Madison, Wis., 1951), pp. 92-93; *Wallace's Farmer,* XLIII (Mar. 15, 1918), 485; (Mar. 22, 1918), 528; (Nov. 29, 1918), 1741; XLV (Apr. 23, 1920), 1206, 1207.

5. *Wallace's Farmer,* XLV (Mar. 5, 1920), 763; (Apr. 23, 1920), 1206; Edwin G. Nourse, *Government in Relation to Agriculture* (Washington, 1940), p. 880; Shideler, *Farm Crisis,* pp. 16-17; Herbert Hoover, *The Memoirs of Herbert Hoover,* Vol. I, *Years of Adventure, 1874-1920* (New York, 1951), p. 243.

6. Hoover, *Years of Adventure,* pp. 276-277, 302-305; Shideler, *Farm Crisis,* pp. 22-23; Walter Weyl, "A Chapter in Wheat," *The New Republic,* XVII (Jan. 11, 1919), 309-311, 320.

7. "Report of the Secretary of Agriculture," United States Department of Agriculture, *Yearbook, 1919* (Washington, 1920), pp. 9-17; *Wallace's Farmer,* XLIV (Jan. 31, 1919), 248; (June 6, 1919), 1217.

8. *Wallace's Farmer,* XLIV (June 27, 1919), 1289; (July 4, 1919), 1321; XLV (Nov. 19, 1920), 2645; XLVI (Jan. 21, 1921), 99.

9. *Ibid.,* XLII (Oct. 26, 1917), 1456; XLIV (Apr. 18, 1919), 893; Iowa Department of Agriculture, *Yearbook, 1919* (Des Moines, 1920), p. 583; Saloutos and Hicks, *Agricultural Discontent,* p. 102; L. C. Gray and O. G. Lloyd, *Farm Land Values in Iowa,* United States Department of Agricul-

ture, Bulletin No. 874 (Washington, 1920), p. 4.

10. George E. Mowry, "The Decline of Agriculture, 1920-1924" (unpublished Master's thesis, University of Wisconsin, 1934), pp. 12-13; *Wallace's Farmer,* XLIV (June 20, 1919), 1256; (Oct. 17, 1919), 2062.

11. Gray and Lloyd, *Farm Land Values,* p. 40; *Wallace's Farmer,* XLIV (April 18, 1919), 893; (Nov. 21, 1919), 2318; XLV (Mar. 19, 1920), 907; (Mar. 26, 1920), 967.

12. *Wallace's Farmer,* XLIV (Feb. 21, 1919), 473; (May 16, 1919), 1065; (June 6, 1919), 1176; XLV (Feb. 27, 1920), 690; (Apr. 9, 1920), 1083; (Apr. 23, 1920), 1207; XLVI (Jan. 7, 1921), 5; (Feb. 4, 1921), 206; Shideler, *Farm Crisis,* pp. 38-39; Saloutos and Hicks, *Agricultural Discontent,* pp. 100-101.

13. Saloutos and Hicks, *Agricultural Discontent,* pp. 102-103.

14. Mowry, "Decline of Agriculture," p. 28; E. S. Sparks, *History and Theory of Agricultural Credit in the United States* (New York, 1932), pp. 444-445; *Wallace's Farmer,* XLV (Jan. 30, 1920), 339.

15. *Wallace's Farmer,* XLIV (Jan. 31, 1919), 248; (Nov. 7, 1919), 2211; XLV (Feb. 13, 1920), 519.

16. *Ibid.,* XLV (July 30, 1920), 1838; (Oct. 22, 1920), 2469; Shideler, *Farm Crisis,* pp. 40-41; *LaFollette's Magazine,* XI (June, 1919), 87.

17. George Soule, *Prosperity Decade: From War to Depression, 1917-1929* (New York, 1947), p. 98; *Wallace's Farmer,* XLV (June 4, 1920), 1511; (Nov. 5, 1920), 2558; (Dec. 3, 1920), 2719; (Dec. 17, 1920), 2788.

18. *Wallace's Farmer,* XLV (Apr. 23, 1920), 1207; (Nov. 5, 1920), 2558; Arthur Capper, *The Agricultural Bloc* (New York, 1922), p. 80; *LaFollette's Magazine,* XI (June, 1919), 120; (Aug., 1919), 122.

19. *LaFollette's Magazine,* XII (Aug., 1920), 125; Herbert Quick, *The Real Trouble with the Farmers* (Indianapolis, 1924), p. 100; *Wallace's Farmer,* XLIV (May 16, 1919), 1065; XLV (Feb. 13, 1920), 519; XLVI (Jan. 14, 1921), 45.

20. *Wallace's Farmer,* XLVI (Jan. 21, 1921), 99; Paul A. Samuelson and Everett E. Hagen, *After the War—1918-1920* (Washington, 1943), pp. 34, 36; *LaFollette's Magazine,* XII (Dec., 1920), 178; *Statistical Abstract of the United States, 1921* (Washington, 1922), pp. 172, 634-635; *The Nation,* CXII (June 1, 1921), 790; Genung, in U.S.D.A., *Yearbook, 1940,* pp. 287, 298.

21. Genung, in U.S.D.A., *Yearbook, 1940,* pp. 287, 298.

per, *Agricultural Bloc,* p. 38; Mowry, "Decline of Agriculture," p. 18; Shideler, *Farm Crisis,* p. 50; *New Republic,* XXV (Dec. 22, 1920), 96;

Wallace's Farmer, XLVI (Feb. 11, 1921), 279.

22. *Wallace's Farmer,* XLVI (Jan. 7, 1921), 5; (Jan. 28, 1921), 150; B. R. Stauber, *The Farm Real Estate Situation,* United States Department of Agriculture, Circular No. 209 (Washington, 1931), pp. 44-45; J. D. Black, *Agricultural Reform in the United States* (New York, 1929), p. 21; Ivan Wright, *Farm Mortgage Financing* (New York, 1923), pp. 9-13.

23. *LaFollette's Magazine,* XII (Dec., 1920), 178; Saloutos and Hicks, *Agricultural Discontent,* pp. 104-105; John D. Hicks, *Republican Ascendancy, 1921-1933* (New York, 1960), p. 277.

24. Gilbert C. Fite, *George N. Peek and the Fight for Farm Parity* (Norman, Okla., 1954), pp. 3-20.

25. Saloutos and Hicks, *Agricultural Discontent,* pp. 111-113.

26. Murray R. Benedict, *Farm Policies of the United States, 1790-1950* (New York, 1953), pp. 171-206; *Wallace's Farmer,* XLIV (Mar. 7, 1919), 588-589; (Sept. 26, 1919), 1853; Shideler, *Farm Crisis,* p. 24.

27. Shideler, *Farm Crisis,* pp. 66-68; Carl N. Kennedy, "The Farmer and the Grain Market," *Wallace's Farmer,* XIV (Nov. 12, 1920), 2605, 2608.

28. *Wallace's Farmer,* XLV (Nov. 26, 1920), 2690; XLVI (Jan. 7, 1921), 4; (Mar. 4,

1921), 412; *New Republic*, XXV (Nov. 22, 1920), 97; XXVI (Mar. 9, 1921), 2; *The Nation*, CIX (Dec. 27, 1919), 815; *Congressional Record*, 66th Cong., 3d Sess., LX (Mar. 3, 1921), 4498-4499; Shideler, *Farm Crisis*, pp. 72-74.

29. R. L. Morlan, *Political Prairie Fire* (Minneapolis, 1955), p. 296; Nathan Fine, *Labor and Farmer Parties in the United States, 1828-1928* (New York, 1928), pp. 389-395; Belle Case LaFollette and Fola LaFollette, *Robert M. La-Follette* (New York, 1953), II, 1001-1010.

30. Shideler, *Farm Crisis*, pp. 34-35.

31. E. G. Nourse, "Agriculture in the Reconstruction Period," *Wallace's Farmer*, XLIII (Dec. 20, 1918), 1861.

Index

tude toward agriculture, 85. *See also* Industry

CABINET, U.S., 4, 11
Capper, Arthur, 76
Chamber of Commerce, U.S.: on open shop, 60; model for agriculture, 82
Christensen, Parley P., 84
Clayton Antitrust Act: business opposition to, 10; labor interpretation of, 34; business opinion of, 37
Coal strike of 1919, 48-50
Comintern influence in U.S., 53
Committee of Forty-eight, 84
Communist party: origins in U.S., 53; raids on, 55; principles, 57; in election of 1920, 84
Comptroller - General, powers, 31
Congress, U.S.: shortcomings, 5-6; class control of, 11; on housing, 13; tax increases (1919), 26; on railroads, 30; on Budget Bureau, 31; follows business leadership, 32; on public works, 36; on tariff, 83
Coolidge, Calvin: on unemployment, 36; on Boston police strike, 43; on business, 62
Cooperative marketing, 83
Corn prices, 70, 78
Cotton, war effects on, 65
Criminal syndicalism, laws on, 52
Curtis, Edwin U., 42, 43

Davis, Harry Lyman, 54
Debs, Eugene V., 58, 62
Deficit financing, 18, 20, 26
Demobilization: of war govern-

ment, 6-7; of Army and Navy, 7-8; lack of plans for, 11; contract cancellations, 12-13
Dewey, John, 9
Duplex Printing Press Co. v. Deering, 61

ELECTIONS: of 1918, 1, 86; of 1920, 62, 84-85
Emergency Fleet Corporation, 19
Espionage Act, Debs on, 58
Europe: U.S. loans to, 18-19; relief needs, 21; purchases from U. S., 22; revival of production, 26; U.S. loans discontinued, 28; needs American food, 68-69; rising production in, 77
Exportable surplus, 81
Exports, from U.S., 21-22

FARMERS' Union, 82
Federal Farm Loan Banks, 73
Federal Reserve Banks: postwar policy, 21; rediscount rates, 26; easy money policy, 73; agricultural policy, 75, 80
Food Administration, 6, 65, 66
Foster, William Z., 45, 47
Free enterprise: cherished by business, 9-10; credited with recovery, 15, 17; demanded as depression cure, 29; vindicated, 32
Fuel Administration, 7, 13, 66

GARFIELD, Harry A., 7
Gary, Elbert H., 46
Germany, purchases from U.S., 22
Gold: wartime accumulations, 21; danger of losing, 26
Goldman, Emma, 55
Gompers, Samuel: war record,

34; advice to, 37; opinions of, 38; re-elected, 39; on Plumb plan, 40; on Boston police strike, 43

Government of U.S.: postwar changes, 6-7; wartime efficiency, 8-9; declining strength of, 11; cancels war contracts, 12-13; postwar finances, 17-18; downgrading of, 32; price fixing, 75

Grange: dislikes Hoover, 66; revival of, 81

Gross national product, 16, 25

HANSON, Ole, 41

Hard, William, 12, 15

Harding, Warren G.: on normalcy, 11; signs Budget bill, 31; appoints Mellon, 32; election of 1920, 62; as President, 86

Hayden, Justice Albert F., 54

Hitchman Coal case, 61

Holmes, Justice Oliver Wendell, 54

Hoover, Herbert: Food administrator, 21, 68; opposes government loans, 28; unpopularity with farmers, 67, 81

House of Representatives, U.S.: defects of, 5; action on Berger, 58

Housing: postwar, 13; new construction, 16; construction falls off, 27

Houston, David F.: Secretary of the Treasury, 11; opposes bond issues, 27-28; influence of, 86

Hughes, Charles Evans, 58

Hylan, John F., 54

IMMIGRATION Act (1917), 55

Industrial Board, 6, 11

Industrial unionism: labor demands for, 38; I.W.W. attitude on, 52

Industrial Workers of the World: Centralia incident, 51; action against, 52-53

Industry: during World War I, 12; postwar problems, 14; revival of, 15; demands on government, 27; compared with agriculture, 64, 78, 80. *See also* Business

Inflation: effect on prices, 24; deflation sets in, 26

Injunctions: Clayton Act on, 34; during 1919 coal strike, 50

Interchurch World Movement, *Report on the Steel Strike,* 47

Interstate Commerce Commission: rate-making power, 40; raises railroad rates, 76

Inventories: overaccumulation of, 22-23; unloading of, 27

Iowa land boom, 70-71

JONES Merchant Marine Act, 7, 30

KUZNETS, Simon, 17

LABOR: business attitude toward, 31; in World War I, 33; postwar, 37; strikes of 1919, 40; in steel industry, 44; American plan, 59; in coal, 48; open shop, 60; in election of 1920, 62; on farms, 74; declining influence of, 85

Labor, Department of, 14

LaFollette, Robert M., 84

Landis, Judge Kenesaw Mountain, 52, 54

Lansing, Robert, 4

League of Nations, 8

Versailles, 2; ineffectiveness of, 5-6; investigates bolshevism, 55
Sherman Antitrust Act, 10
Smith, Alfred E., 58
Socialists: victims of red hysteria, 56, 57; in election of 1920, 62
"Sons of the Wild Jackass," 32
Speculation: in inventories, 22; on New York Exchange, 23; connection with high prices, 24; efforts to curb, 26; collapse of, 27; in land, 70-73
Sproul, William Cameron, 54
Strikes of 1919: effect on business, 22; magnitude of, 40; Seattle general, 41; Boston police, 42; U. S. Steel, 44; coal, 48; occur during prosperity, 59
Supreme Court, U.S.: steel case, 29; Berger case, 58; labor cases, 61-62

TAFT, William Howard: views of the Presidency, 2; as Chief Justice, 62
Tariff: demand for protection, 30; futile for agriculture, 83
Taxes: increased in 1919, 26; demand for lowering, 27; connection with war debts, 28; effect on agriculture, 74-75
Third International, 53
Trade associations, 60
Transportation Act of 1920, 30, 40
Treasury, U.S.: postwar condition of, 18; deficit financing, 20, 25; rising receipts, 26; war debts policy, 28; Secretary Mellon, 32
Trotzky, Leon, 58

UNEMPLOYMENT: curbs urban purchases, 27; war effects on, 34; postwar, 35-36
Union of Soviet Socialist Republics, 53
United Communist party, 54
United Mine Workers, 48-49
United Mine Workers v. Colorado Coal Company, 61
United States: peace loans to Europe, 20; exports to Europe, 21-22; competition from foreign shipping, 26; World War I, 33
United States Employment Service, 35, 36
United States Grain Administration, 21
United States Housing Corporation, 13
United States Shipping Board: postwar changes in, 7; expenditures by, 19; foreign competition, 26; legislation on, 30
United States Steel Corporation: Court upholds, 29; strike of 1919, 44-47

VANDERLIP, Frank A., 20
Vanzetti, Bartolomeo, 56
Victory Loan (1919), 20
Voluntarism, 38

WAGES and hours: wartime, 35; postwar, 41; in steel industry, 44, 46; in coal, 48, 50
Wall Street explosion (1920), 54
Wallace's Farmer, quoted, 64, 67, 79, 82
"War babies," business firms, 12
War debts: expanded after

armistice, 19; demand for repayment, 28

War Department, U.S., 14

War Finance Corporation, 83

War Industries Board: discontinued, 6; on contract cancellations, 14

War Labor Board: activities of, 34; discontinued, 37; protects steel workers, 44

War Trade Board, 6

Washington Agreement, on coal-mining, 48, 49, 50

Weyl, Walter, 12, 67

Wheat: price supports discontinued, 25; war demand for, 65; effects of price fixing, 66-67; Stabilization Act (1919), 68

Wilson, William B., 54, 55

Wilson, Woodrow: idealistic views, 1; illness, 2, 4; in Europe, 3; annual message (1918), 11; advocates public works, 12, 36; vetoes Budget bill, 31; on labor, 33; on steel strike, 46; on coal strike, 49; on agricultural tariffs, 83

Workers' party, 54

World War I: transition to peace, 1; demobilization, 7; economic problems, 9; war contracts canceled, 13-14, 35; comparisons with World War II, 15; Liberty bonds, 17; labor's attitude, 33

"YELLOW dog" contracts, 60, 61